My very best wishes
Daphne Br...

This book is the life story of Daphne Brown who, having as a child survived the war, contracted polio, which affected her spine. She had to wear a spinal brace, and was told by the hospital consultant that she would never be able to work. Against all odds she spent years in multicultural education, 25 as a headteacher, then graduated as a counsellor and worked with the N.H.S. in primary care and voluntarily in a hostel for homeless young people. She travelled widely and developed her own charity raising money for boreholes providing fresh drinking water, in Africa. It is a moving account of hope and perseverance.

I dedicate this book to the many many people who have supported and encouraged me throughout my life, especially the staff and children of Hillshott school in Letchworth and Vivienne, my counselling supervisor and friend.

Daphne M Brown

THEY SAID I WOULD NEVER WORK

Austin Macauley Publishers

LONDON * CAMBRIDGE * NEW YORK * SHARJAH

Copyright © Daphne M Brown 2025

The right of Daphne M Brown to be identified as the author of this work has been asserted by the author in accordance with sections 77 and 78 of the Copyright, Designs and Patents Act 1988.

All rights reserved. No part of this publication may be reproduced, stored in a retrieval system, or transmitted in any form or by any means, electronic, mechanical, photocopying, recording, or otherwise, without the prior permission of the publishers.

Any person who commits any unauthorised act in relation to this publication may be liable to criminal prosecution and civil claims for damages.

All of the events in this memoir are true to the best of the author's memory. The views expressed in this memoir are solely those of the author.

A CIP catalogue record for this title is available from the British Library.

ISBN 9781035895342 (Paperback)
ISBN 9781035895359 (Hardback)
ISBN 9781035895366 (ePub e-book)

www.austinmacauley.com

First Published 2025
Austin Macauley Publishers Ltd®
1 Canada Square
Canary Wharf
London
E14 5AA

Thank you to Marina Rugg, my niece, who has helped me with the final technical details.

Table of Contents

Early Years	11
War	16
Evacuation	21
Polio	29
Boarding School	35
I Would Never Work	46
College Years	50
Hazelwood Lane	54
Madeira	59
The London Emmanuel Choir	63
Change	67
Canada	69
St Mary Magdalene School	73
Win	78
More Changes	82
Sunset	84
Hillshott School	89
Hillshott School Special Memories	100
Hillshott and the Royal Family	106
Life at Datchworth	109

Goodbye	**115**
Bill	**117**
China	**120**
Bulgaria	**124**
Endings	**126**
Zimbabwe	**130**
Boreholes	**134**
Uganda	**142**
Filming Abroad	**146**
A Slight Setback	**149**
The Nursing Care Home	**152**
Harare	**155**
A New Beginning	**161**
Back to Zimbabwe	**168**
Hostel for Young People	**174**
Dogs	**178**
Lockdown 2020	**186**
Over the Rainbow	**191**

Early Years

It was a warm summer afternoon on 2 August 1934. In the neat semi-detached house which stood on the brow of Cat Hill in East Barnet, the grandfather clock struck 4. High above in the front bedroom, a baby's cry was heard; I had come into the world—the firstborn child of Muriel and Victor Brown.

When I was a few weeks old, my parents took me to the New Southgate Baptist Church which my mother had attended all her life. It was Harvest Sunday and the minister—holding me in his arms over a sheaf of corn—prayed a prayer of thanksgiving and dedication. As soon as I was old enough, I went there to Sunday school.

One of my earliest memories was of my toy horse Dobbin, a rocking horse on wheels. I was slow to walk and at the age of two was given Dobbin. Holding tightly on to his red handle, I took my first faltering steps. I cannot recall that moment, but I can remember Dobbin who stayed with me for many years.

Life in those days was simple. No central heating warmed the rooms. The boiler in the kitchen heated the water and coal fires burned brightly in the lounge and dining room. We pierced slices of bread on a toasting fork and held them in front of the glowing flames until they were brown and crisp for tea.

The sweep was a familiar sight, I was terrified of him. I remember so well the day when he suddenly arrived in the yard outside our back door. His bundle of brushes strapped to his back with their wiry heads, and a large sack in his hand. I happened to be standing there, and he grinned at me through his black sooty face. I screamed with fear and ran.

Bedrooms were bitterly cold in the winter. We awoke to the most exquisite fernlike patterns in ice on the windows as we shivered getting dressed. One thing which I really enjoyed was the toilet rolls! Tucked in the tissue were slips of paper containing parts of a story. You had to unwind the complete roll to find out what happened in the end. We then posted all the slips of paper to the makers, and they returned them as a complete storybook.

There were no televisions or computers, only large wirelesses. The main programme we listened to was Children's Hour. This was held from 4 o'clock to 6 in the evening. I loved listening to George Evans who as 'Romany' had adventures with his dog.

'Said the Cat to the Dog', 'Bunkle Butts In', 'Nature Parliament' and the 'Zoo Man', all these programmes gave me great enjoyment and I believe instilled in me a love of nature and animals. Every Easter, *David* would read the story of Oscar Wilde's 'The Selfish Giant'. In our house, this became an annual tradition.

We had to listen and use our imagination with no visual input. One special occasion was when my father brought home a wind-up gramophone, carrying it on his bicycle. There was such excitement. The records were made of vinyl; thin, flat and black, and it was with great care that we laid them on the turntable for they were breakable.

Then, Father wound the handle at the side of the box and the sound of nursery rhymes filled the air, accompanied by a hissing background. What amazing joy, we could actually play the music when we wanted to.

Telephones—if you were fortunate to have one—were tall and black, the sound piece hanging at the side. At one point, we did not have such a luxury, and I used to go down the road with my mother to the red phone box.

She let me insert the coins into the slit at the top of a metal container before, we eventually, got through to the operator who spoke to us personally and then connected us.

I imagine the first three years of my life were reasonably peaceful, but then my brother Gordon was born and life for me erupted. He seemed to cry incessantly and as soon as he could walk there was trouble.

I had a little toy rabbit made out of real fur, which I kept in a wooden hutch in the garden just outside the lounge window. Every morning, I would pretend to feed it, then, one day, it was missing.

Gordon admitted to hiding it, but we never found where, and to this day, I wonder where it went! I also kept some silkworms, which was a popular hobby at that time. Again, Gordon let them all out and put some of them in my doll's house!

However, I still loved him and was proud of my new baby brother as I helped my mother bathe, wash, change his nappy, feed and dress him.

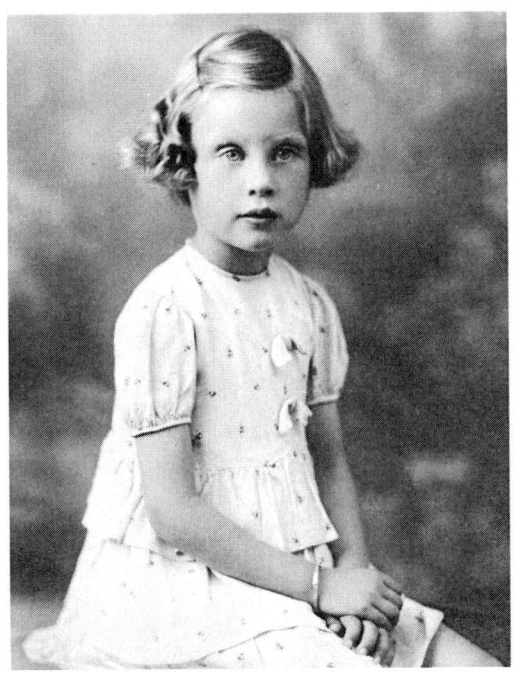

I had a close relationship with my father. He often read me stories from a favourite book, 'The Cow with a Kind Face'. We would go down to the shops and he bought me stencils to draw with and, of course, sweets.

At a very early age, I enjoyed helping him in the garden, even if it was simply picking up stones and putting them in a bucket, or pulling up a few weeds.

During the evening, he would sit by my bed and hold my hand until I went to sleep. Years later, when we had a dog, I was the one who always went with him to the vet. Like him, I loved animals. We had mice that lived in a cage in the garage; a budgerigar which escaped and a tortoise named Billy, who ended his days getting stuck in a fence.

At the age of four, I started school at St Brandon. It was a tiny private school, held in a private house a little way up the road on the opposite side.

The head teacher was Miss Hope and her sister, Auntie Meg, gave us hot milk to drink in thick china mugs at break time (there were no plastic cups in those days!). Miss Oram was the only additional teacher.

I was dressed to go on the first day. My mother had bought me a new pair of shining patent shoes, the soles were smooth and slippery; one step at the top of the stairs and I crashed down the whole flight. I left for this new adventure sobbing my heart out!

I enjoyed school, although, I found learning to read from the Janet and John books difficult.

I always enjoyed Christmas and my parents never failed to make it a very special occasion. One of my earliest memories was waking up on Christmas morning and seeing a large box on the foot of my bed.

Opening it carefully but with huge excitement, I was greeted with the face of a warm cuddly panda. I still have him now. He was special because in 1936, the first panda to leave China was taken to America, and then, in 1938, four pandas arrived in England. One was named Ming. So, it was, that toy pandas were created and mine was one of the first.

I loved my dolls and my doll's pram. Sadly, however, there was a major problem. The majority of dolls had china heads. They only had to be dropped once and their heads would be shattered. Glass eyes were fixed with wire between two holes, and sometimes, the eyes fell out leaving two staring gaps.

The dolls' hospital was kept incredibly busy and many a tear was shed by the owners. I remember visiting an aunt once. I had a beloved doll in my arms, as I reached for the doorbell, I dropped my treasured possession and she lay in pieces on the doormat. I sobbed and sobbed and sobbed. Today's plastic does have its advantages.

There were two dolls, however, who played a major part in my life and I still have them. One was Peggy. She had a Bakelite head and a stuffed material body and thus survived my childhood. Although her nose is broken, she still retains her wonderful smile. My other doll Rosemary is very precious. She was given to me by my grandmother and had previously belonged to my auntie Beeche. I never knew this aunt as she died from diphtheria at the age of 19, and Rosemary had been her childhood companion. Rosemary is a beautiful doll and still has a pride of place in my sitting room.

She has an enchanting, tranquil china face, original authentic blonde hair and double-jointed limbs. I have several sets of clothing which came with her, the most relevant is a dress and bonnet made from muslin which—I presume—was the fashion 140 years ago when she was created in Germany.

My father had taken over the family civil engineering business Biggs Wall and Co. named after my great uncle and grandfather. At one point, he was responsible for erecting all the street lighting in the Isle of Wight. He always sent me postcards when he was over there, and I still have them in an album today.

As soon as I was old enough, he took me with him. I loved those visits; going on the ferry and playing with the slot machines when we arrived. We had two proper holidays as a family in Mundesley, Norfolk.

Life was happy. Those early memories, shine with beautiful moments of joy and contentment, security and peace.

Then, everything changed.

On 3 September 1939, Germany marched into Poland. My parents sat huddled around the wireless, and the war was declared.

War

As a five-year-old, it was not possible to comprehend the full implications of war, but I quickly picked up the anxiety of my parents, especially from my mother, whose brother had been killed in the terrible 1914–1918 conflict.

My first apprehension was my mother making heavy black curtains and hanging them in all the rooms creating dark shadows during the day and total blackness at night. They changed the character of the whole house. But, even at that early age, I understood their importance and significance in protecting us from enemy action.

During the night, wardens would patrol the streets, and if there was a light showing, even the tiniest glimmer through a crack between curtains, they would either bang at the front door or blow a whistle. I heard a whistle one night and ran barefoot into my parents' bedroom, crying.

The next procedure was sticking strips of sticky tape across the glass of all the lounge (sitting room as it is called now) windows to prevent them from shattering if they broke from the blast of a bomb. Finally, large blocks of turf were piled up against the frames, completely shutting out the daylight.

My and Gordon's beds were moved down into this room for safety. I developed measles and as the doctor recommended keeping me in a dark room, I lay in bed looking at the layers of turf and the black curtains. My mother gave me the very last tin of orange segments from the cupboard. This delicacy would not be seen again for at least five years—rationing had begun.

Every person was issued with a ration book, and before long, everything was rationed apart from vegetables. Fruit from abroad was non-existent. After the war, when eventually bananas arrived, I didn't know you had to peel them and I tried to eat the skin!

To begin with, on 8 January 1940, bacon, butter and sugar were rationed. Then in 1942, meat, milk, cheese and cooking fat. Each week, one adult was allowed 1 egg, 2 ounces of tea and butter, 1 ounce of cheese, 8 ounces of sugar, 4 ounces of bacon and 4 ounces of margarine. Then, for me, the most important item was 12 ounces of sweets every *month*.

We had points in our ration books, and I would save mine until the last Saturday of the month. Then, I would go with my father to the sweet shop and spend them. It was one of the major treats in my life, and I so looked forward to it. There were no ice creams.

Before the war, one of the daily attractions was the ice cream man pedalling his three-wheeled bicycle and ringing his bell. He had a freeze box attached to the front which held just vanilla cornets, wafers and orange ice lollies, but these were a real treat to the children who ran out to greet him. He was sorely missed.

There were ways of supplementing the food rations legitimately, although the black market was rife. Meat was limited according to availability. My mother had heard that rabbits were coming into the butchers. I was sent down to wait in a long queue. While I was standing there, I noticed a £1 note lying on the floor in the sawdust.

£1 was the only paper money at that time. I think several people saw it, but no one wanted to risk losing their place in the queue. However, I stepped out and picked it up! When I finally reached the counter, I paid for my rabbit and then handed in the note.

To my delight, I was given a sixpenny coin as a reward. I was thrilled, I can remember it so clearly to this day, that sixpence meant so much. I ran all the way home—the rabbit in my arms and the sixpence in my pocket—I could hardly wait to tell my mother.

She had to try and make the very best of rationed food. We had cakes made out of carrots and iced with dried milk and dried eggs to name but one item. Often lunch was gravy made from boiling up the bones of a chicken when we had been fortunate to get one.

Incidentally, even the fur of the rabbit was not wasted. Mother made them into gloves for me as clothes were rationed from 1941 to as long as 1949—five years after peace was declared. All my dresses had previously belonged to my cousins. As soon as they had outgrown them, they were passed on to me. From 1940 to 1947, the government organised British Restaurants to provide simple hot meals for children and needy people. I went to one for lunch on a number of occasions.

We had prepared for an onslaught of bombs almost immediately, but for some time, nothing happened and then we heard it—the air raid warning. Still, to this day, 80 years later, my heart misses a beat if I hear that sound on the television.

I cannot remember whether the first one was during the day or the night, but I do recall so clearly, my mother grabbing Gordon and shouting at me to get under the kitchen table—with a mixing bowl in her hand!

There we crouched together until—after what seemed to be hours and hours—the *all clear* went and we emerged from our hideout. Many, many times I ran, terrified into my parents' bedroom when the siren whined its way through the night air. It was then, that I began to shake.

Whenever there was an air raid, I physically shook and trembled, no amount of reassurance or cuddles could rectify this. I was unable to stop myself, no matter where I was, or whether it was day or night. I shook from head to toe.

We were all provided with gas masks. Mine was housed in a pale pink case and I had to carry it everywhere when I went out, including taking it to school. Gordon had what they called a *Mickey Mouse* variety. It had large goggled eyes and ears and was bright red whereas mine was black.

One comfort was our neighbours. Three ladies, known to me as Auntie Alice, Auntie Win and Auntie Olive. Our house was semi-attached to theirs and, whenever, there was an air raid they would knock on our adjoining wall and we knocked back.

A simple gesture, but so meaningful during those times of fear. Sadly, for us, these friends moved to Southbourne, a short while after the war started.

Even in those early days, I saw frightening evidence of the danger surrounding us. During one night, a bomb fell just a short distance from our house, shattering a number of our windows which fortunately remained intact thanks to the sticky tape.

In the morning, my father took me down the road to see the crater and the dentist's house which was virtually destroyed. On another occasion, I watched from my bedroom window as a house blazed on fire; the flames—ignited by incendiary bombs—lit up the night sky.

The blitz began in London. Although I was only six years old, my mother stood me on the kitchen table to see the vast glow of flaming orange across the sky as London burnt in agony due to the horrific bombing.

Every morning, I would go out into the garden and pick up pieces of shrapnel, bits of metal, broken off shells and bombs dropped by the German planes that had flown overhead. I still have those pieces safely preserved!

If there was an air raid during the night, we were allowed to go to school one hour late. When an air raid occurred during the day and we were at school, we all crammed into the front room where—in a similar fashion to my house—turf blocked the windows. I learnt to knit during those occasions!

My parents decided that it was time to purchase an air raid shelter. They chose the Morrison indoor model, and the excitement when it arrived was overwhelming. Father slowly pieced it together. A large, very heavy, brown metal table-like structure, with metal latticed sheets that hooked on all four sides making it like a cage.

It was quickly equipped with sheets, blankets and pillows, and replaced our beds in the lounge. That was where Gordon and I slept from then on throughout the war. Thankfully, he did not seem unduly worried about my shivering and shaking during the air raids.

We stopped attending the Baptist Church which was some distance away, and instead, went to the local Congregational Church, just a short walk across a field from where we lived. My father became the Sunday School Superintendent.

Religion played a large part during my childhood, and some of it was very strict due to my mother's puritanical upbringing. We were not allowed to play games on a Sunday, and I could not even do knitting. My father never did any gardening on this day and certainly, my mother would not even consider doing any clothes washing, that was completely out of the question! All the shops were closed, it was treated as a quiet day with many people attending church.

One strong memory I have was a Toy Sunday. This special day was held just before Christmas when all the children in the church were asked to bring toys. These were then put on or beside a Christmas tree and afterwards taken to either Dr Barnardo or the National Children's Homes.

Toys were very scarce during the war, many that were given to me were second-hand, and I found it hard to decide which one I should give to the toy service. My Mother suggested a dog, but I loved this dog. She was called Bessie and had white fur and grey ears.

I was told that children who had no toys at all needed her. I carried her across the field to the church, crying all the way and, finally, parted with her. Every night I knelt by my bed, eyes closed and hands together, then recited.

"Gentle Jesus, meek and mild,
Look upon a little child,
Pity my simplicity,
Suffer me to come to Thee.
Amen.
God bless Mummy, Daddy and Gordon.
Amen."

I am not sure how much those words really meant to me!

Evacuation

As far as I remember, the word evacuee meant nothing to me. I cannot recall any preparation for what was about to happen.

I imagine, I must have been told that our former neighbours: Auntie Alice, Auntie Win and Auntie Olive had phoned my parents and suggested that I should go down to stay with them in Southbourne, away from the London bombing, and my parents had agreed.

I only know that one morning, I was standing in the hall and there was a knock on the front door. A tall lady stood on the doorstep—oh she looked so large, so enormous—dressed in a brown uniform which I later learnt was the outfit of a land army member.

She introduced herself as Auntie Annie. I cannot recall ever saying goodbye to my mother, father or Gordon. But I clearly recall walking down the front garden path, holding her hand and clutching a little case; my gas mask strapped around my shoulder.

Did I even wave goodbye, I wonder?

My next recollection of that day was Auntie Annie pushing me into a train carriage packed with soldiers, then—asking them to look after me—she left. The train moved off.

There was no indication of where we were going as all the names of the stations had been removed for safety should there be an invasion by the German army. Suddenly, the train came to a screeching halt. There was a massive commotion and I was surrounded by shouting.

A soldier grabbed me and I was pulled from the carriage onto the nearby platform and told to lie on the floor face downwards. A siren was whining up and down, a plane screamed overhead and the sound of bombs echoed through the air.

Then, suddenly everything went silent. I lay on the ground with prostrate soldiers all around me. I was only just six years old, but I can still remember the details, and feel the fear and bewilderment as if it was yesterday.

After what seemed to be hours, but I am sure it was a comparatively short time, an *all-clear* sounded. We got up and I climbed back into the carriage, and the train continued its journey. Finally, I arrived at my destination, Southbourne.

The train stopped, soldiers opened the door for me, the driver came and checked that I was disembarking, and there on the platform were my three aunties: Auntie Alice, Auntie Win and Auntie Olive. I was safe.

My *aunts* did everything they could, to help me adjust to my new surroundings. We went for beautiful walks. Auntie Olive took me across the fields to Christchurch. Masses of marsh marigolds were cushioned alongside the water's edge, and pontoon bridges were being constructed and tested in the estuary for war use.

We frequently walked along the road by the sea, but barbed wire was stretched across the whole of the coastline due to mines being buried in the sand in case of invasion. I never once had the chance to run on the beach or splash in the waves.

Auntie Win and I used to wander to the inland countryside. She was the one who taught me to look and listen. We stood one day by a field of mustard, its brilliant yellow glowing in the shining sun.

I can hear her words now, "Daphne, let's just stop and look. I want you to remember this beautiful sight, so that, if ever you are feeling sad or worried, you can remember it and it will cheer you up."

We stood for a few moments in silence. How true, I have never forgotten that precious moment. She often stopped me to listen to the birds and, in particular, the wood pigeons.

"Listen, Daphne, it is saying, 'Take two pears, Tommy, take two pairs, Tommy'."

How true. Every time, I hear that call, I think of her. When I returned home, I stood for hours by our kitchen door, watching a bluetit by a hole in the garage roof where it had made its nest.

I counted the number of times in an hour it flew in with food for the babies and sent a letter to the local paper with the results. To my delight, I was awarded half a crown, two shillings and sixpence. The gift Auntie Win gave me of treasuring nature has remained with me for the whole of my life.

I slept in the corner of Auntie Alice's bedroom. As I lay there in the early hours of the evening, I would listen to the music coming from their wireless downstairs. The signature tunes of 'Much Binding in the Marsh' and 'In Town Tonight', still ring in my ears—I loved them.

One sound which scared me, however, was the wind whistling in the telegraph wires. I hated it, and then, of course, there was the occasional air raid warning. This very rarely happened locally, but the distant sound of sirens coming from Poole Harbour filled me with fear.

Auntie Olive was very much aware of how I felt and saddened by the way in which I was trembling and shaking with alarm. She tried everything to calm me down, including cuddling me, in her arms.

And, if it was during late evening or the night, taking me into her bed and holding me with her soft hands—they were so gentle.

Slowly, I would relax and realise that the warning was a long way off and no bombs would be falling on our house.

One evening, I was sitting downstairs in my nightdress, drinking a cup of hot milk before I went to bed. The wireless was on, and we suddenly heard the voice of Princess Elizabeth and immediately stopped to listen, "I feel that I am speaking to you as friends and companions who have shared with my sister and myself many a happy Children's Hour. Thousands of you have had to leave your homes and be separated from your fathers and mothers."

"My sister Margaret Rose and I, feel so much for you as we know from experience what it means to be away from those we love most of all. To you, living in new surroundings, we send a message of true sympathy, and at the same time, would like to thank the kind people who have welcomed you into their homes."

"It will be for us, the children of today, to make the world of tomorrow, a better and happier place. My sister is by my side and we are both going to say *goodnight* to you. Come on Margaret. Goodnight children, goodnight to all of you and good luck to you all."

I turned to my *aunts* with a huge smile of amazement:

"The Princess was talking to me; she knows how I feel."

It meant so much.

A picture that I often looked at in my *aunts'* home, was a large portrait hanging on the wall by the stairs. It looked to me like an elderly man with a long white beard. I soon learnt who he was, and my *aunts* would sit with me on the stairs and tell me about his life and adventures.

His name was Hudson Taylor, he was their uncle and the first missionary to go into the interior of China. He worked there for 51 years until 1905 and founded the China Inland Mission—which today is known as the Overseas Missionary Fellowship.

Hudson Taylor was renowned for discarding his black English tailored suit—which was the attire of missionaries at that time, and gave him the name Black Devil—and instead, wore a long Chinese gown while growing his hair into a plait.

Aunties had one of his gowns and I, very carefully, dressed up in it one night. It was beautiful, dark blue silk with delicate, intricate designs woven into the material. Years later, it was left to me in their will, and in turn, I have now given it to the Overseas Missionary Fellowship.

So, it has gone back to where it belongs. I was fascinated by all the stories I heard about this man and China, and later in life, they played a part in two meaningful experiences.

My *aunties* were members of the local Methodist Church, and every Sunday, we worshipped there. I joined the Sunday school and was awarded a certificate for collecting donations towards the Junior Methodist Missionary Society. They were happy occasions, I felt loved.

During the week, I attended St Mary's Gate Private School, a short distance from where we lived, travelling each day by bus. It was, of course, much larger than the little school I had been used to at home, and I was the only evacuee child there.

But they made me very welcome and I enjoyed it. In a letter which I sent home, and my mother kept and eventually passed on to me, I wrote.

'It is simply *grand* at school. I have 14 girls in my class and I am quite friendly with one already, her name is Daphne Parker and she is in my class as well.'

'All the teachers are nice except one, her name is Miss Smith and she really is a nuisance! I can do purl in knitting now and am knitting some gloves without any fingers, only a thumb.'

Eventually, there was a lull in the bombing and I went home for a short while, only to return again a few months later. This time, an uncle drove me down and I was able to take with me my beloved doll Rosemary. As time went on, I returned home on several occasions.

It was hard and unsettling going back and forth between two schools, the little private school at home and the larger one in Southbourne. My work was affected and friendships were difficult to maintain, but it became a routine.

Each time, I was transported either by car driven by a friend or on the train escorted by a land army lady. Sometimes, it was Auntie Annie, and at other times it was Auntie Daisy whom I had met at Southbourne; never again did I have to endure the traumas of my first journey alone.

In spite of my young age, I was very aware of some of the atrocities that were being experienced throughout the world, especially those concerning Jewish children. My mother came into the kitchen one day and found me kneeling on the floor with my head in the oven.

"Whatever are you doing, Daphne?"

"I'm trying to see what it's like to be gassed," was my muffled reply.

When I was at home, I enjoyed going on the bus alone to my maternal grandmother. I loved her dearly and would sit for hours cleaning her brass and just talking. I appreciated her pictures on the wall.

One was of the composer George Frederick Handel—when he was a little boy—secretly playing the harpsichord up in the attic. A lady was coming through the door holding a light followed by his father who had forbidden him to play. This painting sowed a seed in my life.

I have always had an interest in childhood composers, and many years later, shared it with countless children in school. One of the greatest gifts my mother gave to me was the love of music. She had a beautiful singing voice and would listen for hours to classical concerts.

I started having piano lessons at the age of six, and sometimes, even practised during an air raid as the piano was in the lounge with the blocked windows. Every time I returned home from evacuation, I continued with lessons, and the joy of playing the piano has remained with me all my life.

At a very young age, I asked for a recording of Tchaikovsky's piano concerto to play on our wind-up gramophone. My wish was granted, and I received the appropriate set of black vinyl discs.

Even today, when I hear that piece of music, I recognise the various points where we had to stop and change to the next record in order to continue. Sadly, I had only had this precious gift for a few days, until I accidentally knocked one of the records and broke it. What a difference compared with today's Alexa!

One evening, when I was just getting into bed, my mother told me that another baby was going to be born in our family. In those days, there were no scans, and pregnancies were almost hidden by voluminous dresses—it was a secret!

David arrived that very night in the same room where Gordon and I were born. I heard nothing and was then told in the morning I had a new brother. Still, in my nightdress, I tentatively crept in to see him—such a tiny baby lying in the same cradle as Gordon had.

I held his little hand and hoped he wouldn't be frightened by the war. A private nurse came and stayed for two weeks; the length of time my mother remained in bed. Nursie—as we called her—also cared for us. Every night, she tucked me into bed and read me the story of 'A Peep Behind the Scenes'.

In June 1944, I was almost 10 years of age and now living at home as my *aunts* were moving to a small bungalow. When not at school, I enjoyed helping my mother in taking care of my brothers. Then, one night we heard it!

A loud deafening bubbling, grumbling sound, vibrated through the darkness and grew louder and louder and louder until it seemed to be just above the roof of our house; everything shook, it continued, then suddenly stopped, silence then, a huge explosion—the Doodlebugs had come.

They were a terrifying invention. An unmanned bomb which came at any time of day or night without any warning. No sirens sounded and you were at their mercy. Then, suddenly, they would stop.

There would be this ominous silence, a terrifying pause, and then, it crashed and exploded. I lay in the shelter with Gordon and we would hear one coming in the distance. Nearer and nearer.

I closed my eyes and fearfully thought, *In a few minutes I shall know what it's like to be dead.*

The noise stopped and we waited and then heard a huge crash—it had missed us. We wondered who had been hurt as we breathed a sigh of relief.

It was midnight. I was sharing a bedroom with Gordon when we, suddenly, heard the most enormous hum of planes. We jumped out of bed and stood watching through the window in amazement as hundreds and hundreds of planes flew overhead.

On and on they went throughout the night, we could not make out what was happening, so we just stayed watching. A few hours later, we heard about the horrors and success of D-Day.

I was told that, once again, I was going to have a new brother or sister—oh, how I hoped it would be a sister. This arrival was more meaningful for me. I could see my mother was pregnant there was no secrecy and I enjoyed helping to prepare for the new baby. Then more excitement, we were going to move house.

Our new house in Winchmore Hill was large and detached in a quiet crescent, away from the business of traffic. The garden spread out for nearly two acres and a huge chestnut tree adorned the first lawn. I loved it. An outside air raid shelter was neatly tucked in one corner.

I had to change schools and was sorry to leave St Brandons. That little school had been a haven for me during all those confused, fearful years; it was hard to say *goodbye* to the friends and staff whom I had grown to love and trust.

My new school was very different and I knew no one. As I walked home, I was often bullied by boys who stood in front of me and would not let me pass—it was not easy.

8 May 1945, the day we had longed for came at last. VE celebrations were held everywhere and a street party was organised in our crescent. I still had no friends of my own, but I enjoyed it.

Heather was born three weeks later in my parents' bedroom. I waited expectantly in the garden with my father and brothers. Nursie was there again.

She called out of the window, "It's a girl!"

I was so delighted to have a sister and was one of the first to hold her. She had a shock of dark hair and I cuddled her so carefully in my arms.

Nursie watched me. "Maybe, the next baby you hold will be yours," she said.

It was not long before I wheeled Heather out in her pram. I met a girl who lived just three doors away, but we had never spoken.

"That is a nice brother you have," she said, peering into the pram.

"It's not a boy, it's a girl," I replied indignantly. "She is my sister!"

From that moment onwards, Jan became my friend and we remained so for 76 years!

The following year we had our first holiday in years. We went to Norfolk and stayed in an uncle's caravan. I was 11 years old and had not had a holiday since I was four. The barbed wire had been removed from the beaches and the sand cleared of mines.

We arrived late on Saturday evening. As soon as breakfast was over on the following morning, I asked if I could go down to bathe in the sea.

My mother firmly replied, "No, it's Sunday, you must wait until tomorrow."

I pleaded for her to let me go, but she was adamant, no swimming on a Sunday.

My father then intervened, "Let her go."

Finally, my mother gave way. For the first time in my memory, I joyously ran across the sand in my bare feet and into the waves only to trip over a rock and severely cut my knee!

Limping back to the caravan, I was taken to the local Girl Guide Red Cross Centre and duly bandaged, but sadly could not go into the sea for the rest of the holiday!

My mother quietly commented, "God was punishing you."

I had the scar on my knee for the rest of my life.

Polio

After a year, I moved schools again, this time to a girls' private school Palmers Green High School. I was much happier.

Then, my friend Jan started at the local grammar school, Southgate County. We thought it would be good if I could join her there. So, after some private coaching, I took the 11+ examination and went with her.

During that period, poliomyelitis was rife. It was a life-threatening disease which often caused severe paralysis, especially of the legs, diaphragm and muscles around the spine. It was especially prevalent with children; many had to be placed in an iron lung while they slowly recovered, and sadly, some died.

Shortly after I went to Southgate County, I began to feel poorly. I felt extremely tired and had an incessant pain beneath my left shoulder blade. My mother kept telling me to go to bed earlier, but I refused! David then caught chicken pox and, as was the custom in those days, the doctor came to visit him.

My mother said, and I can hear her words now, "While you are here, you had better take a look at Daphne's back, she keeps complaining about it hurting."

At that point, she left the room while I removed my dress and vest.

The doctor prodded my spine and asked, "Can you feel that?"

"No."

He called to my mother and said, "Look, her spine is twisted and she has no feeling in the centre, no wonder she is in pain."

My mother just stood there in shock.

"Has she at any time had a form of influenza or something similar during the past year?"

"Yes," my mother replied, "but that was some time ago, and she wasn't ill enough to call you."

The doctor paused then continued, "I think Daphne has had a mild attack of polio which has affected her spine and, possibly, other parts of her body. She is getting the pain under her shoulder blade because that is where she still has some feeling and the spine is pressing on it."

"I want you to take her to the Royal Orthopaedic Hospital in Great Portland Street tomorrow, I will make an appointment for her to see a specialist."

The doctor left, my mother cried, and I got dressed.

The following day, we took the underground train to Great Portland Street and the Royal Orthopaedic Hospital. I was examined by a consultant whose name I believe was Mr Paton, and he confirmed that my spinal curvature and paralyses of the muscles were caused by polio.

I was taken to be measured for a spinal brace. This was similar to a large corset, but its design was very different. The metal rods were about one inch wide and stretched from my neck down to the very base of my spine. There was hardly a gap between them.

They were inserted into stiff, coarse, linen-type material which I fastened in the front with large buckles. Thick leather straps were attached at the top to go around my shoulders ensuring that the support was held in a permanent upright position.

The following week, I went with my mother to collect my brace and was also introduced to the physiotherapist. She gave me a selection of exercises which I was told to do daily after removing my brace, and then, she put a rubber-like collar around my neck and under my chin.

This was attached to a rope hanging from a stand, which she pulled until my feet were lifted off the ground. I was then left dangling in the air for several minutes before being lowered down again. The purpose of this was, of course, to try and straighten my spine.

My main memory of the procedure was the vibration in my ears and the extreme clenching of my teeth. I visited the hospital every Saturday for physiotherapy, and soon, became familiar with the journey so went on my own.

From what I remember, I accepted the brace without too much difficulty. This was partly because there was a certain amount of relief.

I no longer had pain under my shoulder blade, and the brace held my back up, where I had previously felt a weakness that I could not explain. At last, a solution had been found, for many months I had felt something was wrong.

The two things which I objected to were: having to do a series of exercises every evening after I took the brace off, and having to have a dressmaker make my clothes. My cousin's clothes no longer fitted.

My parents found it difficult to come to terms with the situation.

When I protested about doing the exercises, my mother would cry and plead with me saying, "You must, you must, otherwise, you will have a humped back when you are older, please…please try."

Even slight physical deformities were hard to accept. Queen Victoria's first grandson was hidden during his childhood because his paralysed left arm was deformed at birth. He was still living four years before I had polio. The word for a person who had difficulty in walking was a 'cripple'. A local charity that tried to support them was John Grooms Crippleage—a far cry from the Paralympics of today.

Apart from the conversations over my exercises, the bi-monthly appointments with the consultant and the dressmaker's visits, I cannot remember ever talking to anyone about my back, or saying how I felt both physically or emotionally, it was as if the problem did not exist.

My father never mentioned it and my mother became upset if I referred to it for any particular reason, but inwardly, I was not happy.

Having been to three different schools during the three previous years, I had not made any permanent friends apart from Jan Then, little disadvantages began to occur because of my back.

I became increasingly frustrated having to have all my clothes made. They were old-fashioned, and even though clothes were still rationed, new designs were coming onto the market and one of them was *slacks*. During the war, siren suits were provided for ladies, something quick to put on when there was an air raid.

Now, they were no longer needed, *slacks* were introduced, and these first-time trousers for ladies became the fashion. All the girls were buying them, but none would fit me.

I remember hopefully trying on jodhpurs at a horse-riding shop, but could only pull them up as far as my hips! I longed to go out to the shops and choose something pretty to wear.

This has always been a problem and I have to continually remind myself that clothes are not the end of the world.

As I grew older and fashions changed, I did manage to buy loose outfits that fitted, and that was always the criterion when I looked in a clothes shop; I could never choose something just because it was pretty. It was years before I finally found trousers that would fit.

Shoes were another difficulty. Because of my spine, one leg became shorter than the other and I had to have my left shoe raised by thickening the sole. This meant that all my footwear had to be flat, I have never had a pair of shoes with high heels.

My problem with clothes was not only frustrating for me, I know it disappointed my mother. She loved beautiful clothes and always dressed with great elegance. My parents could afford to buy anything for me to wear, but they just would not fit!

I managed to do most things, but one experience does remain in my memory. We had a hard tennis court at the end of our garden, and my parents held tennis parties for their friends, mainly people from the church. Although I played my own fashion of tennis with my father, it was rather hit-and-miss as I could not lift my arms above my head. So on these social occasions, I would stay in my bedroom and watch through the window. Everyone arrived in their white outfits and then enjoyed refreshments afterwards.

I did not seem to mind missing out on this, but it would have been more enjoyable if I could have joined in. Life began to feel very lonely.

It is relevant at this point—I think—to give a little insight into the background of my home and family. My parents had a privileged upbringing which filtered into our way of life.

We had a maid named Mary who came from Ireland and lived with us; a lady whom we called by her surname Mrs Brown and who undertook light duties such as sewing, preparing the vegetables etc.

Miss Geddes did the cleaning and George was the gardener. I was known to all of them as Miss Daphne. Our large garden was beautiful, my father's pride and joy.

For three consecutive years, he came first in the London Royal Horticultural Society's competition for private gardens, where a gardener was also employed. Having won three times, he was no longer allowed to enter.

My parents were extremely particular about the type of person I mixed with. My mother frequently used the word *refined*, and if a friend did not fit into this category, then I could not comfortably bring her home. Margaret was one.

She had been confirmed in the church and I had a photo of her in her white dress; surely she would pass the test! She came home to tea and afterwards, my father took her back to where she lived.

When he returned, I was told that she lived in a terraced house and was really not our *class*. There were others too, who, for one reason or another, were considered unsuitable for me to have a close relationship with. I totally disagreed.

I cannot recall any comments about my back at the grammar school. The brace was obvious. If I leaned my head and neck forward, it stuck out under my clothes, and I was permanently rigid. I was excused from taking part in P.E. and games, which I was quite pleased about, otherwise, life continued as normal.

It may have been the reaction to my parents' views, or possibly polio that gave me a concern for others with a disability, but there were two girls whom I always tried to sit next to in the various lessons—because I felt sorry for them and they were bullied.

One had terrible eczema and the other had permanent nits in her hair. A lovely thing happened with the latter girl. Many years later, I attended a missionary conference, and she was one of the main speakers—what a special and privileged reunion that was.

At that time, we as a family, attended Oakwood Baptist Church and there was one member who was a great support to me, Gwen Baker. She had been a missionary in China, employed by the China Inland Mission, and could hardly believe it when I told her I had been evacuated to Hudson Taylor's nieces.

Gwen invited me to her home for tea on many occasions. We had long conversations about China and I became more and more fascinated with this country; she had to leave very quickly when the Japanese were invading.

18 months passed at the grammar school, but I became restless. Mother was occupied with my brothers and sister, and I imagine I was still having difficulty in settling in from having been away from home intermittently for so long, from the age of 6 to 10—such formative years.

My parents did not approve of my friends, and I argued with my father who, in my opinion, treated me like the younger children! He was reprimanding me one day and stretched out his hand.

I thought he was going to hit me, so I ducked and fell off the chair onto the floor, then couldn't get up because of my back. My mother shouted at him as she tried to help me onto my feet again, and there was such a commotion as the other children all joined in.

Disabilities can affect every member of the family, and each one reacts in a different way. I was constantly aware of this, and consequently, outwardly tried to pretend there was nothing wrong.

If my mother did occasionally offer help, I would promptly refuse it. I even tried to persuade her not to come with me for my bi-monthly appointment with the consultant, but she insisted on being there.

Like the majority of children at that time I enjoyed reading books written by Enid Blyton. One of my favourites was 'The Naughtiest Girl in the School'. I identified with her! Boarding school sounded exciting. One evening, my father came home and said, he had been to my school. To this day, I never knew why, but he saw graffiti on a wall.

He was disgusted. Shortly afterwards, he and my mother spoke to the neighbours who lived opposite, about the boarding school their daughter attended—Berkhamsted Girls School—and they decided to send me there. With Enid Blyton's description of such a place, I happily agreed with the arrangement.

Boarding School

The day arrived, when once again, I was leaving home. A large metal trunk had been extricated from the loft and packed to capacity, we then set off in the car.

I had visited the school twice. Once, when I took an entrance exam, surprisingly I passed, and on the second occasion, when we visited the second-hand clothing shop! That was a total embarrassment for me. My mother knew that it was pointless to buy a ready-made uniform that would never fit.

In consultation with a member of staff, it was decided to purchase a selection of second-hand outfits and have them altered by the dressmaker according to my needs.

I had to try on so many garments, none of them fitting, but finally, a choice was made and the necessary adaptations were applied. The one item I could buy and wear was a loose baggy blue school pinafore which we wore over our uniforms presumably to keep them clean!

I was in the Loxwood House and my bed was in the blue dormitory. Both my parents came in with me and helped me unpack, then, they left and I was duly introduced to some of the girls.

Looking back, I have often wondered how my parents really felt; sending me away again, separating me from my brothers and sister, and knowing I had this back problem.

However, I regularly wrote letters home and my mother kept them and passed them on to me. They reveal the true story, and I am, therefore, printing some in considerable detail.

Here are excerpts from the first one I wrote, about a week to 10 days, after I arrived:

'The girls in my dormitory are ever so nice, there are six of us. Ray is the head, she is *wizard*. On Saturdays, there are buns and coffee or lemonade in the dining room and we can go in and help ourselves at any time, it's lovely. I saw the doctor yesterday with the other new girls.'

'He didn't say much only that I was to continue with my exercises. I also had my eyes tested by reading some letters at the end of the room, I rattled all the letters off and both the doctor and sister said I had excellent eyesight and that very few people can read to the end.'

'We went blackberrying on the Common last week and yesterday we went hipping for rose hips to make rose hip jelly. The Common is miles and miles of grassland and bracken with just a lonely farm or two. We scrambled through bracken (ferns) as high as ourselves and went home with bags of hips to a hot bath and a lovely meal of salmon pie.'

'The hips go to a nearby hospital and there is a cup awarded to the house that gets the most hips, Loxwood got it last year, and I hope we get it again.'

'You know Nature Parliament with Uncle Mac on the Children's Hour when children can send up questions on nature, well the man who speaks on animals in that programme came and gave us a lecture yesterday evening. He was ever so interesting.'

'He told us that he lives in a house with his sister and snakes, cats, dogs, bats and a badger. They all have the free run of the house. He told us that apart from monkeys etc. animals are colour blind. Afterwards, we were able to ask questions.'

'I have enclosed my sweet coupons as we aren't allowed to use them, please, send me some sweets.'

'Every evening juniors, middles and seniors lug me to the piano and make me play either my own pieces or sight-read theirs. They say I'm the best sight reader in Loxwood and the best player for my age. I don't mind playing in front of anyone now, even Matron.

'We had just come in from our Sunday walk and I and a few others, seven altogether, got lost and we didn't meet the prefects and Matron in the right place. In the end, we went home by ourselves. Matron was very nice about it.'

'I must finish now as the letters are just going to the post and it is hymn practice.'

'With much love Daphne.'

What a difference! How positive, I was happy. I was free to enjoy life without my back problem interfering. Even the doctor, obviously, did not make an issue of it and focused on what was good—my eyesight.

I scrambled through bracken with my friends no one was worried about my back, and then, they encouraged me to play the piano. I am sure that no one at my last three schools even knew I could play, and yet it was something I could do which was not affected in any way by polio.

Each letter I wrote throughout all the years I was at that school, was full of joy, everything was *super* and I am going to quote a number of them later.

I would have thought I would have been embarrassed undressing in front of the six girls in my dormitory, but I cannot ever remember feeling awkward at any time. They just accepted me as I was. A few helpful exceptions were made.

Every morning, it was the practice for all the girls to run around the garden before breakfast! I was quietly given permission to be exempt from this as it took me time to put on my brace, no one made a fuss, and I was pleased not to have to run! I especially appreciated one incident. A mobile vehicle for TB screening came to the school. We all had to queue up and wait our turn.

When it came to mine, the radiographer gave one look at me and said, "You will have to take that thing off."

I was so embarrassed, but the girls immediately came to my rescue. They formed a circle around me—hiding me from the view of all outsiders and anyone looking in through the windows—while I unstrapped and removed my brace, had the x-ray taken, and then dressed again.

I could never thank them enough, and even now, as I write, my eyes fill with tears at the memory of their quiet care and concern for me.

During morning assembly, I found it difficult, nigh impossible, to sit cross-legged on the floor. Instead, I was allowed to sit on a chair in the gallery beside the organ.

Every evening, I did my exercises in the dormitory with the house mistress checking on me. It was important for me to continue them as I no longer went to the orthopaedic hospital for physiotherapy.

The only comments I remember were the girls feeling sorry for me having to do this, but they made no fuss. At one point, the consultant suggested that I should have a board put on my bed to keep the mattress firm and straight.

The school caretaker found a suitable board in an air raid shelter and sawing it down to the right size, fitted it onto my bed.

A few excerpts from my letters home:

'Last Wednesday, we went over the RMS Carthage. One of the girl's father works for the P&O liners. It was huge…two officers took us around. It had a cinema and a dance hall.'

'We went into the first-class cabins, and bathrooms, in fact, we went all over the ship including the games deck and swimming pool and both the tourists and first-class lounges. At 5 o'clock, we had a lovely tea (free) in one of the first-class lounges.

'Waiters helped us off with our blazers, and pulled our chairs in and out as we sat down. We each had our own teapot and milk jug, and when our plate of cakes was empty it was whipped away and replaced full again before you could say, *Jack Robinson*.'

'The waiters were dressed in white and they stood perfectly straight and still by the tables, until they saw you wanted something.'

'We had a marvellous day yesterday. There were some great tennis matches against St Margaret's school, the first team lost but the second team won…in the evening, the leavers and some of the staff acted in a Sherlock Holmes play in the garden.'

'Then, we had a terrific tea/supper, but I really felt sick. I couldn't eat another chocolate biscuit, plates of fruit salad, cheese straws and a great bowl of sweets, there were tons left over.'

'Then, from 9:30 to 10:10, the whole house yelled the latest songs around the piano (me playing), while Matron and Johnny (housemistress) did all the washing up. Then, at 10:15, we ended up with Auld Lang Syne.'

'We had a fete in aid of the church organ fund with an awful lot of stalls…I put my foot in it as I took over the treasure hunt stall, and yelled out to all the boys to come and have a go.' "Come on have a go, you've got plenty of money, surely, you can pay sixpence."

'But actually, they hadn't. They were from the local orphanage and their master gave me such a look. The other night we were caught eating strawberries in the dorm, but we didn't get into much of a row.'

'Last Monday, we had a very interesting day; we went to Oxford. We went over Maudlins College, Bodley and St John the Baptist College. Then, we had a picnic by the river and afterwards, went to Trinity College and Christ's College.'

'We then went to a cafe and had iced lemonade. We then went to the cricket match where the Australians declared 297 for two and we were all out for 107! However, it was quite good.'

'Dear all, I'm alive I hope you are. I've had no letters this week, disgusting.'

'Dear all, I'm having a super time, the monitors have suggested I have a little plot in the garden for my own as I love gardening.'

'Dear all, I am still here! We went for a walk along the canal this morning···Last Monday, we had a half-holiday as it was the Prince's birthday. We had a marvellous time mucking around until tea. Then at 4:30, we went over to the school hall and danced with the other boarders till 6:30.'

'Then, came supper. Matron was dreadfully decent. She spent her afternoon preparing a supper of poached eggs on toast and huge dishes of fruit salad and cream for us. It was wonderful…I joined the GTC (Girls Training Corps) last Friday.'

'We went on a scavenger hunt in groups. Each group was given a slip of paper with 60 different things we had to find; these are a few of them: a sultana, two bus tickets which add up to 6p, a beech, oak, cherry silver birch, and lime leaf, the menu at the King Arms.'

'I am in a smashing dorm *yellow* with Anne, who is dreadfully nice; Tatty, who is also wizard, and Dingle, who is the head, and is awfully nice. She gave Tatty and me a peppermint cream last night—even though she was head and sweets aren't allowed in the dorms.'

And so, the letters continued. It is interesting to me to see the emphasis on food. We had so much more choice which were luxuries now that rationing was slowly coming to an end—although we still had ration books until 4 July 1954, and this was only 1948–1952.

Every letter was positive, and my back—apart from one reference to the exercises—was never mentioned.

My parents were also extremely supportive. We had a visiting day every third week and they often came and took me and any friend I chose, out for tea at the Kings Arms Hotel. Gill frequently came as her parents lived in Cornwall, and Jane from Beccles also joined us on occasions.

On some visiting days, I actually returned home for the day, and mother prepared a wonderful tea shared by all the family and my friend Jan.

I was, at times, slightly rebellious. Instead of saying grace before the evening meal, we would sing a hymn. I was responsible for taking hymn practice on a Sunday evening, and accompanying the hymns when we sang them.

On a number of occasions, Miss Johnston (Johnny) the housemistress, would tell us to cut out some of the verses. I felt this was wrong, so, I told the girls that I would play all the verses and, hoped, they would sing them—and they did! Johnny—as we called her—spoke to me and we agreed to choose short hymns!

One of the popular things at that time was to have a penfriend; someone of your own age living in another part of the world. I was linked with a girl called Lucy. She lived in Jacksonville, Florida. I continued to write to her for over 60 years until there was finally silence.

While I was at boarding school, she sent me a huge box of assorted chewing gum. Johnny said I could show it to my friends, but they were not to have any, as only 10 sweets sent from home were allowed each week, and chewing gum was forbidden. I could not resist letting everyone have just a taste of the contents.

At supper, Johnny announced, "Anyone who has had any of Daphne Brown's chewing gum is to come to my room after supper."

There was a queue along the hall and right up the stairs—everybody came! We had no jam or cake for a week as a punishment. Johnny took the box away.

However, she returned it to me on the last day of the term to take home. During the holiday, I packed up some of the gum and sent it to her as a present! I'm not sure whether she appreciated it. I believe she thanked me.

A group of us decided to have a midnight feast. We asked some day-girls to buy food for us (as boarders were not allowed to go to the shops) and we secretly smuggled it in. Some of us prepared a room in the attic. We crept upstairs after the lights were out, covered the windows with blankets, and then, laid the food out on the bags they were brought in.

It was a true Enid Blyton occasion, but we forgot about maintaining silence. At about 2 o'clock, we returned to our dormitories. In the morning, those of us who took part were summoned to the headteacher. This was serious.

You only went to see the headteacher by appointment, and very rarely in her office. We were each given a specific time by the secretary and called separately. I remember silently waiting outside her door—alone, wondering what she was going to say.

I went in and she asked me if I had taken part in the midnight feast, I said yes. She did not waste words but told me that if this happened again there would be no more similar activities as I would be sent home—not to return.

The thought of being expelled filled me with horror, it never did happen again! We discovered that a member of the kitchen staff had a bedroom in the attic, she heard everything that was going on and reported us!

One event took place after I had been at the school for about two years, just a simple experience, but something which had a profound effect on my life. We were due to go home for a week's half-term break.

Unfortunately, one of the girls developed scarlet fever, so we all had to stay in quarantine. The way the staff cared for us was amazing.

We played card games with them, and the different treats we were given to eat and enjoy, were exceptional—bearing in mind rationing was still enforced. We could get up when we wanted to and stay up until 10 in the evening. There was a wonderful casual atmosphere, and fortunately, no one else caught scarlet fever.

Nevertheless, it was a disappointment not going home, and one person I missed seeing was Gwen Baker, my ex-missionary friend from church. I wrote her a letter explaining what had happened.

A few days later, I received a reply, and she wrote:

'Have you given your life to the Lord Jesus? There will be many disappointments that you will have to face throughout the coming years, but if your life is in His hands, the Lord Jesus will always be there to help you, love you and give you strength and peace.'

'This little prayer from a hymn will help you.

Just as I am without one plea,

But that thy blood was shed for me,

And that Thou bidst me come to Thee O Lamb of God I come.'

I read the letter over and over again. I had been taken to church every Sunday since I was born, and even during my evacuation had attended Sunday school.

At boarding school we went to Matins—the Sunday morning service at the parish church—it was just part of life, but it was always because somebody expected me to go. I began to quietly think, how much did Jesus Christ mean to me personally?

The quarantine was over and we returned to our usual school routine. We were allowed home for a long weekend to make up for the half-term we had missed. During that time, in the silence of my bedroom, I quietly prayed the prayer in Gwen's letter. A few weeks later, I was baptised by immersion in the local Baptist Church we attended as a family.

When I returned to school, I automatically assumed I could now go to Sunday morning communion with the girls who had been confirmed. I mentioned this to the housemistress. She then queried it with Miss Russell the headteacher.

There was obviously a problem with the vicar who was only comfortable with giving communion to those who had been confirmed. I will never forget the wisdom and understanding of Miss Russell.

She sent for me and asked if I would like to go to the Baptist Church for evening communion once a month. I readily agreed. I can still remember her words as she enquired as to whether I minded going on my own, or did I know a day girl who went to the Baptist Church.

I didn't and so she arranged for one of the church deacons to come and fetch me and take me to the appropriate service every month. This was a real privilege and I was so grateful.

The school was very particular about health safety especially when we returned home for the holidays, and they insisted on having an *entertainment policy*.

If there was a general epidemic of an infection such as measles, then we were told not to go to any places of entertainment during our stay at home. My parents strictly adhered to this ruling, but I thought it was ridiculous! I remember, during one holiday the film Odette came to our local cinema.

Odette was held in high esteem by me and many of my friends. She had worked in France with the underground movement against the Nazis and was captured and tortured, but survived. I pleaded with my father to let me go and see it, but he quite firmly refused, in view of the school's ruling.

He promised to take me if it ever returned. Years later, the film did come back to the area, my father kept his word, and we went and saw it together.

Summer holidays were now a treat following the long weary years of war. My parents took us every year to Woolacombe in North Devon. We stayed in a little guest house where we were the only family.

I loved the vast stretch of sand and expanse of the sea without any barbed wire, and the joy of eating sandwiches in our beach hut was quite special. However, my favourite occupation was something completely different. The owner of the guest house had a severely disabled daughter called Shirley.

Shirley was the same age as I was. She could not speak and was unable to walk or even sit up. She went out in a long wheel chair which was similar to a bed. One of the first things I did when I met her was to ask if I could take her out. Her mother was so surprised at my offer, no other guest had ever done this.

I would take Shirley out every morning, disregarding the looks of passers-by, while the rest of the family, built sand castles and bathed in the sea!

Every holiday was the same, I always looked forward to seeing Shirley and enjoying our outings together. Then, one day, I received a letter at school. Shirley had died.

I was devastated. I tried to write to her mother, but could not find the correct words, I had never had to send a message to a bereaved person before, I just did not know what to say, so I decided to write a poem:

'She was like a tiny tender flower,
With petals closed up tight,
Which only God could open,
In His heavenly home so bright.
We loved her, but He loved her more,
Beyond the farthest measure
And so, she went to be with Him,
Our precious little treasure.'

Shirley was buried in Morthoe Cemetery, on the headland which overlooked the sea. The words of my little poem were carved on her tombstone.

I continued to visit the Royal Orthopaedic Hospital during each holiday for a check-up, and also to have my brace adjusted according to how much I had grown.

After three years without regular physiotherapy, it was considered that my condition had deteriorated and the consultant advised further treatment at the hospital, once a week. This initially caused confusion and concern.

Would I have to leave school and attend somewhere else in order to fit in the necessary hospital visits? Once again, the school was extremely cooperative. Although there were no weekly boarders, they agreed for me to be an exception. I was allowed to go home every Friday evening and return on Sunday.

At first, I thought this was a great idea, but I soon realised how disruptive it was. Leaving my friends on Friday and missing out on all the weekend activities at school. Then, getting up early on Saturdays to travel on the underground train to Great Portland Street for vigorous physiotherapy at the hospital and finally, going back to school on a bus the following Sunday afternoon. I was physically exhausted and the weekends were so disjointed, all the school and home activities were disrupted and I felt I was missing out on both. This continued until I finally left school.

My time at Berkhamsted was coming to an end. It was the last year for taking the School Certificate before it changed to the G.C.E. and I did not do well. Having taken five subjects, I only passed in three.

Miss Russell sent out the details during the summer holiday and on mine, she wrote:

"I am afraid you will be disappointed with these results!"

(I retook the two failures at Christmas and passed!)

On our return for the autumn term, the form teacher asked us to write down what career we were hoping to take up when we left school.

I wrote, 'I want to be a mother with six children.'

She passed the piece of paper back to me saying, "That is not a career!"

It was 6 February 1952. Miss Russell summoned everyone to the hall—something was wrong. I went up to my usual seat on the balcony and looked down on the whole school waiting in anticipation. Miss Russell entered and stood in her usual place on the platform, there was a pause.

"Last night, our King George VI died quietly in his sleep. We shall be thinking of the Queen Mother and the two princesses especially Elizabeth who is now our Queen."

A silent sadness engulfed the hall like a heavy blanket. We left shocked and returned to our classrooms.

As I write today, the world is tossed in the confusion of the coronavirus epidemic. Zoom meetings have suddenly become the norm, and through this medium, I have met up with four of the *girls* who were boarding with me; we had no contact for 70 years! Jane, who used to come out to tea on visiting days, and Nancy, Margaret (Randy) and Barbara who were in my dormitory, were all younger than I was.

Barbara still had the poem I wrote for her to wish her well in her exams. She sent me a copy, then sadly, a few weeks later she died. It was a strange completion of a circle of life, sharing our youth, then years of silence and at the final end, being suddenly together again to say "Goodbye".

"Barbara you do expect a lot,
I've tons of things to do,
Besides just writing poems,
To a little, girl like you,
But I will just wish you all the best,

And hope you get on well,
Now remember, don't take books to bed,
Or rise before the bell.
And as I've said to Randy,
If you do your very best,
Your parents will be proud of you.
Because you stood the test,"
Thank you, for all the happy memories we shared together.

I Would Never Work

It was the Easter holiday and all the girls in my year were planning for a future career. I wanted to work with children. I was not highly academic, but with my experience of helping to care for my brothers and sister, I felt this was something I could do.

I went with my mother for my three-monthly check-up at the Royal Orthopaedic Hospital. Lying on a bed in a cubicle the consultant examined my spine, he then closed the curtains as he spoke to my mother. Although I was 17 years of age, I was not included in the conversation but, of course, could hear every word that was said.

The consultant explained that as I had almost stopped growing I could be transferred to a local hospital and reduce my physiotherapy.

He then continued, "You must accept that she will never be able to work, she will be unable to stand or sit for any length of time without pain and will fail all medicals, and she will always be a problem for the dressmaker."

My mother asked, "What about her getting married?"

"If she has any children they will probably be deformed during pregnancy because of her spinal curvature."

These words still ring in my ears as if they were said yesterday.

The consultant continued speaking with my mother, but all I could think of was: *She will never work and her children may be deformed.*

The curtains were suddenly drawn back, and I stood up and dressed. No reference was made to this conversation apart from the consultant shaking my hand and saying that he was referring me to another hospital. We returned home. My mother never mentioned to me what she had been told, and I never let on that I had heard every word.

I was determined to continue with my idea of working with children. I had a friend who was a house mother in Dr Barnado's home, so I asked if I could visit her at Barkingside. I returned home full of enthusiasm and sent off an application to become a house mother.

My parents made no comment one way or another. I had to complete a medical form, polio was mentioned, and almost by return, I received a letter to say I had failed. I applied to a Missionary Society where one of our church members had a sister, who worked in North Africa.

They both suggested I might like to go and help care for orphaned children in Casablanca. I loved the idea, but my parents both opposed it; my father was particularly against it.

"There are plenty of children in England who need care."

I continued with my application and was told that a room had been prepared for me in Casablanca; it was painted yellow, and I just had to have a brief interview and a satisfactory medical report from the doctor. I failed the medical report because of polio.

I then applied to a number of teacher training colleges, but everyone sent the same response when they saw my completed medical form:

'I am sorry but we are unable to offer you a place due to the fact you have had polio and it has physically affected you.'

I returned to school for my final term. All my friends were looking forward to either continuing their studies or going to university or college. I was left wondering what to do. I had only passed five subjects at the O level standard and had even failed two of those and had to retake them.

It was a warm summer evening. As usual, I had gone to bed an hour earlier than everyone else as it was felt I needed extra rest. I lay there listening to the girls playing tennis just outside the window. Their voices and laughter rang through the still air as the balls thudded back and forth.

I kept thinking of what the consultant had said. What was I going to do? I so wanted to get married and have children of my own. I felt I had missed out on family life with evacuation and boarding school, but would any man want me with a spinal brace and the complications which could arise if I became pregnant?

I lay there thinking. Then, I had an idea. God may have someone in mind for me, so in spite of the difficulties, I would start praying for that person—whoever and wherever he is—and that is what I did.

Every night from then onwards, I prayed for the person who would one day be my husband, so that, when I met him, I could tell him how much and how long he had been in my prayers.

The end of term was coming, and with it the highlight of a dance at the boys' school. All the dresses for the occasion were arriving and hung around the dormitory on coat hangers hooked to the picture rail.

The final evening arrived, and the girls dressed with excitement and much delight, especially as they were allowed to wear makeup. They finally left in the transport provided. I went to bed and lay looking at the empty coat hangers; I would never have the joy of dancing, I could not wear a ballroom dress and I could not feel anyone's hand on my back.

At 10 o'clock, the girls returned having had a fantastic time. Dancing is a joy which physically disabled people are often deprived of, but even that is being overcome today as a profoundly deaf and also blind person have both won 'Strictly Come Dancing'.

One thing that really stands out, at this time, is my faith. In spite of all the consultants, my parents and the various organisations had said, I was convinced that God had a plan for me and all would be well.

With this in mind, I applied to the local Teacher Training College, Trent Park. My parents advised me not to, as once again I would be disappointed, but I went ahead.

The application forms came through, one containing medical questions. I completed them and awaited a reply. it came; I had failed the medical! I can remember having a sense of calm rather than disappointment and frustration. The end of term arrived at school, and as the tradition was, we all queued up to say a formal *goodbye* to the headmistress.

I recalled her kindness to me and thanked her. Then, she wished me well on my teacher training course, and I had to tell her I had failed the medical, so would not be accepted; they were my last words to her.

I returned home, and a few days later, received a letter inviting me to attend for interview at the college. My parents said I should let them know I had failed my medical questionnaire, but I was determined to go and see what happened.

I waited patiently outside the principal's office and was then invited in. No one else was in the room. I can see his face even now; a white-haired quite elderly gentleman with a firm but kind face that spoke of wisdom and experience. He asked me a number of questions and then said they would offer me a place on the infant training course.

I just looked at him and said, "Thank you, but I have to say, I failed the medical report because I have had polio."

He looked straight back at me, I will never forget his words, "You look as if you've got willpower, we will accept you!"

I do not know to this day, whether the medical report had failed to reach him, or whether he had read it and was willing to give me a chance. I will forever be grateful for his understanding and trust in me.

College Years

The training course at Trent Park was only two years long because, although it covered every aspect of teaching, it was counted as an emergency course in order to qualify as many teachers as possible following the war.

Obviously, it meant a great deal to me because of the circumstances surrounding my appointment. But it was also a huge change from being a boarder at a Public Girls' School and, also, once again, living permanently at home.

The infant lecturer, Miss Armstrong was excellent, and I related to her well. Those of us who were training for infant teaching met in a Nissen hut left over from the war. We were separate from the students working with junior and senior-aged pupils.

I loved my first *teaching practice* at Bounds Green Infant School, and felt so at home with the five-year-old children, that I knew I was in the right place and doing the right thing.

One aspect which I still found extremely difficult was *clothes*. The wartime clothes rationing had now completely stopped, and the students were relishing the joy of going to the shops and being able to buy just what they chose, without any restrictions.

The suppliers made the most of this and a wide variety of fashions flooded the market. I went to see what was available but, of course, nothing fitted. It was many years later when I was working as a qualified teacher, that I bought the first dress which could cope with my brace.

Shoes were still a problem because of the raised sole on my left foot. This was easy with the shoes I had worn at school; they were flat with one strap. Now, at college, everyone wore high heels or wedges. I had to stay with my old flat shoes and one sole thicker than the other.

Every day, I walked along a drive from the entrance of the estate to the college—a narrow lane about a mile in length. Unfortunately, one of the students was badly attacked in this region and my parents were concerned about my safety.

Much to my absolute delight, they bought me a Vespa scooter. I just loved it. My friend Jan had a Lambretta, and we often went out for drives together. Eventually, we decided to drive as far as Dorset and visit my evacuee aunts who now were living in Sherbourne. It was quite an adventure, but we made it!

Music has always been important to me. At the age of nine, I played the hymns for our school assembly, then continued lessons at boarding school, and reached the seventh grade with the Royal Academy. Now, at college, I chose music as my specialist subject.

I continued having lessons privately with a delightful teacher, Miss Lownds. She was a tiny lady, beautifully dressed, with her hair neatly tied in a velvet ribbon. She became a great friend of mine. I soon was prepared to take grade eight, and for this, I had to go to the Royal Academy in London.

I was called into the room, but as I went to sit down at the piano, I fainted with nerves. The examiner was extremely kind. He helped me get up from the floor and escorted me outside asking someone to fetch me a glass of water.

After resting for a while, I returned to the room and, this time, took the exam; playing the chosen pieces and answering the required questions on theory.

When the results arrived, I had been awarded a merit!

Another aspect of music which meant a great deal during my college years and later, was the concerts my mother took me to. Every year, she entered the ticket ballot for the last night of the proms. She ordered a large number and was always successful in obtaining some.

I was unable to go when I was at school, but now, I was free to join her and friends—how I loved those occasions.

The atmosphere was, and still is unique, with the playing and singing of the Sea Shanties, Rule Britannia, Pomp and Circumstance, Jerusalem and finally Auld Lang Syne. In those days, Sir Malcolm Sargent was the conductor, he always wore a white carnation.

I joined the college's Christian Union. At that time, Gladys Aylward—a famous missionary who had worked in China and rescued a hundred children during the Japanese invasion (The film The Inn of the Sixth Happiness with Ingrid Bergman portrayed her life story)—had returned home and was living in Tottenham.

Because of the interest I had in China, I contacted her and invited her to come and speak at one of our college Christian Union meetings. She was a very challenging person, and I took a great interest in where she was working and the church services she was taking part in. I often went with her.

Gladys was very short and when she was preaching she would take a box with her to stand on, so she could see over the pulpit. My job was to carry the box.

I well remember how—when we were travelling on the underground train in London and passengers were smoking—she would stand up and address all the travellers as if they were a congregation—demanding them to put out their cigarettes.

She would then tell them how she had seen children working in the tobacco fields in China, and how cruel it was. Amazingly, the smokers, nearly all men, would extinguish their cigarettes. I admired Gladys enormously, and treasure the letters I have from her, some with her Chinese signature.

I really enjoyed my first year at Trent Park. I was sure, that in spite of all the consultant had said, I would be able to cope with a teaching career, and I loved working with the children. Then, just at the beginning of the second year, I was rushed into hospital with appendicitis.

I should have only stayed there for a week to 10 days, but when they operated they found my womb was completely reversed and further surgery was needed. This incidentally, had important implications 70 years later! I was a patient for six weeks, and then needed time to recuperate.

It was decided to change my specialist subject from music to art, thus, enabling me to work at home. I finally returned to college two weeks before Christmas, just before receiving a letter suggesting I stayed on an extra year. Fortunately, this was not necessary.

During the following Easter break, we had our first family holiday abroad which involved the new experience of flying. We went to Switzerland and stayed in Lucerne. My two outstanding memories are the bridges containing the most beautiful paintings, and going up Mount Rigi three times.

The first two visits were shrouded in dense fog and the view was obliterated, but it was worth making a third attempt; the clear magnificent scenery above the clouds was amazing, and truly awe-inspiring.

The final term came all too quickly. A second *teaching practice* took place in Tottenham with a very fierce head teacher (Miss Armstrong felt I could cope with her!) and then it was *goodbye*. I was sad to leave as I had made some good friends, but we agreed to keep in touch. A few weeks later, I received my teaching certificate—I had successfully passed!

Hazelwood Lane

When I left the college, there was a policy to offer teaching places to students in local schools, without them having to apply. I was given the choice of Hazelwood Lane Infants in Palmers Green, which, I accepted.

Setting off on that first morning riding my Vespa, I experienced mixed feelings of both apprehension and excitement. I had only visited the school once during the holiday, simply to meet the headteacher and see my classroom.

Hazelwood Lane School consisted of an old established building, housing three hundred children between the ages of five and seven.

The Headteacher Miss Hughes was a little lady of about five feet in stature, who knew every child personally by name, and ran the school on very strict formal lines. This was extremely helpful to me as a probation teacher, with much to learn.

I had a reception class of 40, newly arrived five-year-olds, who sat side by side in rows of dual desks throughout all the teaching hours. The three R's: Reading, Writing and Arithmetic were paramount and on every Friday morning, Miss Hughes would come into my room and give the children a spelling test of 10 words, which I had hopefully taught them during the week. One piece of equipment that I thought belonged to another era—long ago—was slates.

Every child was issued with a little slate and a piece of chalk. This may have seemed old-fashioned but it was, in fact, very useful. Writing could be erased without any difficulty and words copied off the blackboard with ease.

On Friday afternoons, the children were allowed to paint a picture or play with plasticine as a reward for their spelling efforts; their only art *lesson* of the week. Our one other occasion for a slightly more relaxed time together was enjoying music.

Because I played the piano, I took a number of singing lessons and was also asked to take hymn practice with the whole school. At first, I found this somewhat daunting, but it was a good experience. I counted it a privilege, and as time went on, it became something to look forward to.

I had only been there a month when I was asked if I would mind taking in one more child; a little boy whose mother was ill. This made a total of 41 children in my class, but feeling sorry for him, I agreed.

As teachers, the only additional help we had was one *welfare helper* for the whole school. Her responsibility was to mix up powdered paint for every class and care for any child who had been hurt or felt unwell.

The school was very quiet. There was no talking as the children moved between classrooms and cloakrooms before walking out to the playground. When it was time to come in, Miss Hughes would ring a large handbell at the main door.

Silence immediately ensued and continued as the children lined up class by class. The boys would then pause to take their caps off (they all wore school uniforms) before entering the building and cloakrooms, then, finally back to their desks, when they were allowed to speak.

One little incident which comes to my mind and makes me smile. My classroom was adjoining the hall. I was talking to the children about quietness and the importance of listening.

"Let's see if we can hear the birds," I suggested, although the sash windows were closed and this was probably impossible.

The children fell silent. The sound of a teacher's voice echoed through the nearby hall and a little voice piped up from the back row of desks, "All I can hear is a parrot!"

In spite of the strict regime, there was a lovely atmosphere in the school. I personally appreciated knowing exactly what I should be doing and what I was aiming for. I think, the formal atmosphere also gave the children a sense of security.

The staff were extremely supportive, but there was one slight unfortunate incident. I received my first salary and looked at the amount with surprise, it was much more than I expected.

The deputy head also received her regular salary and found that, for some reason, it had suddenly been reduced to almost half the amount. Her name like mine was Miss Brown! The mistake was quickly rectified and it was decided that I should adopt an additional name to avoid any further confusion.

I chose *Vernon* after a distant relative of mine who established several residential homes for children suffering from mental and social difficulties. From then onwards, I was known as Miss Vernon-Brown which I preferred and kept for many years.

Under her seemingly strict countenance, Miss Hughes had a heart of gold. She just wanted the best for the children and she cared about her staff.

I had only been in the school for a short while before she noticed, how difficult it was for me to get down to the small low cupboards, in fact impossible. Without any fuss, she asked the caretaker—as far as he could—to raise all the cupboards higher, which made it so much easier for me.

The children had also noticed my spinal brace sticking out under my clothes when I tried to bend over to talk to them. They asked me quite seriously if it was where I kept my books!

At this time, I was particularly concerned, and indeed bewildered, by the aggressive attitudes between certain church denominations. The school welfare assistant was a Seventh-day Adventist and we used to spend time during the lunch hour, discussing our ways of worship and linking them with the Bible.

Looking back, I wonder how I ever found time to do this and am not surprised that Miss Hughes also queried as to why we were meeting regularly in my classroom. She was a Roman Catholic, and I explained to her how confused I was about the divisions between denominations.

I told her about Bridget, a lovely friend I had at college who was a Roman Catholic. I had invited her to our church carol service and she wanted to come, but her parents and her priest forbade it and my parents too told me I should never have asked her. Bridget was also interested in our Bible study group, but again, I realised she would not be accepted.

I could not understand why a nonbeliever would be welcomed and a Roman Catholic turned away. Miss Hughes took the time to listen to me—even though it had nothing to do with school—and she told me her brother was a Catholic priest and she would arrange for him to meet me.

A few days later, I was invited to their house. I cannot recall our conversation, but I well remember him asking me at the end to kneel down on the mat in front of the fire and we said the Lord's Prayer together.

I valued the conversations we had in the staff room; they were wide and varied. The school secretary talked a great deal about her holidays in Alfriston, a beautiful historic village in Sussex. She recommended a guest house and my friend Jan and I stayed there for a delightful week. It was the first time that I had been on holiday without my family.

The first year came to an end and in doing so heralded my 21st birthday, 2 August 1955. In those days, 21 was the important coming of age not 18. My parents were very generous and wanted to make the celebration special.

I was able to invite friends from boarding school who were within travelling distance, friends from college, friends from church, members of staff from the school, and my parents even contacted the headmistress of the little private school I had attended during the *war,* and she too was able to join us.

My mother went to tremendous lengths preparing a wonderful tea and making most of the delicacies herself, but my biggest concern was what was I going to wear. I searched many shops, but there was nothing that would fit.

I had almost given up when, in despair, I finally went to a tiny boutique without any hope, and there was a beautiful blue/grey silk dress—exactly what I wanted. I went into a cubicle half-heartedly to try it on, but it was impossible to even pull it over a fraction of my brace. I was virtually in tears, what was I going to do?

To my utter amazement, the owner of the shop came into the cubicle with a tape measure. "Let me see what I can do."

She measured me in all directions and asked, "Would you like this dress?"

I could hardly get the words out, "I would love it, but it is impossible."

"Nothing is impossible, leave it with me."

I returned a week later. There it was, and it fitted! I kept that dress for years and years and will never forget the kindness and ability of that shop owner.

It was a glorious day, the sun shone, the sky was blue and all my friends gathered in large and small groups throughout the garden. The tea was laid out on one of the lawns, everything was perfect apart from one tiny incident which left me bewildered for a moment and has stayed with me ever since.

Miss Armstrong my college tutor was one of the guests and she was talking to my father.

I was nearby and could not help hearing what they were saying:

"Daphne has coped so well with her back, hasn't she?"

To this, my father replied, "There is nothing wrong with her back, she is fine."

Realising I had heard his response, Miss Amstrong came and spoke to me, "He likes to think of you as someone without a disability, doesn't he?"

All I could answer was, "Yes."

For my second year, I was given a class of slightly older children aged six to seven. I was working with them one afternoon and happened to glance out of the window—to my utter disbelief I saw my father walking across the playground.

He had never been in the school before and I could not imagine why he was there now. Had something dreadful happened? He disappeared into the building, and uncertain as to what I should do, I just carried on teaching; I could not leave the children!

As soon as the bell rang for playtime and the children had gone to get their coats, I hastily made my way to Miss Hughes' room. She called me in, my father had left. He had recently been quite ill with throat cancer, but thankfully, he had responded well to treatment and the prognosis was good.

Miss Hughes invited me to sit down and explained that he had just returned from the consultant who had advised him to have a few weeks in a warmer climate. Having discussed it with my mother over lunch, they felt Madeira would be very suitable.

But my father would need someone to go with him, and my mother would have to stay at home to care for the younger members of the family. Miss Hughes said she had agreed for me to have a leave of absence until Christmas, so that, I could accompany him.

I could hardly believe what I was hearing and was somewhat surprised that all this had been discussed and decided without me. The prospect was exciting and it was decided that I should leave at half-term.

Madeira

The day had arrived for us to set off on our journey. It was decided that my younger brother David—who had been suffering from severe bronchitis—should join us.

We boarded a train from London to Southampton, but on arrival were told that the flying boats to Madeira were not able to leave due to the stormy weather. We then travelled 44 miles to Blackbushe Airport and climbed into an old wartime Dakota plane, hoping to fly to Lisbon in Portugal.

The weather worsened—and frantically tossed by the elements—we made an emergency landing at Bordeaux airport. My father and David were vomiting as we staggered into the airport waiting room where we remained until the following day.

The storm slowly abated and once again we set off. Although continuously tossed from side to side, we finally arrived in Lisbon where we stayed in a hotel for three days. My one memory of this capital city of Portugal is the cork trees; they fascinated me and I still have the sample someone kindly cut off from a bark.

On the third day, we made our way to the harbour where a flying boat plane awaited our arrival. Unlike today, there was no airport in Madeira, and the only way of reaching the island was by sea.

It was an amazing experience to land on water with such speed and force. There tiny boats came out to meet us and take us ashore in Funchal.

We stayed in the Miramar Hotel, situated in the shadow of the famous Reids Hotel which stood elevated high up above us, on the overhanging mountainside. Our residence was small but very welcoming, and we soon made ourselves at home.

There was colour everywhere, and each morning, a flower girl would stand below the window offering a posy of brilliant flowers for sale. My father rested for much of the time and David spent hours in the swimming pool where he was taught to swim by a man with just one leg.

The island was beautiful with open water channels, known as Levadas, flowing for miles alongside the roads and lanes, irrigating the vegetation and the tiered cultivated valleys overlooked by high majestic mountains.

It was not long before I met a lady whose room was not far from mine. She introduced herself to me very quickly and I soon learnt that she was indeed a titled lady, Lady Bee Chater.

Although Lady Chater owned three castles in England and flew her own plane, she always spent the winter months in Madeira and had her own private suite. When she heard why I was there and realised that I was not a normal tourist, she took me under her wing—what a privilege!

The local people had great respect for Lady Chater and wherever we went, they would often kneel down in the road as she passed by. It was fun sledging together down the steep narrow streets in a wicker toboggan where men pushed us with great speed along the sloping surfaces.

Lounging in colourful hammocks, we were individually carried to different places of interest.

In the evenings, we listened to the music of Chopin and other classical composers as Lady Chater played her records on an old wind-up gramophone. The sound may not have been perfect, but I thought it was beautiful as we sat listening to the music and watching the sun setting over the sea.

I was able to talk to Lady Chater in a way in which I had never been able to converse with anyone before. I shared with her my thoughts on marriage and how I was praying for my husband every night; I felt able to tell her about some of the difficulties I was experiencing with my back.

She really listened and seemed to understand, which was such a help. She assured me that I would get married one day and gave me hope.

One morning, Lady Chater said that she wanted to take me to meet someone. We set off in her chauffeur-driven car to—for me—an unknown destination. It was not long before we reached an outcrop of rocks embedded with caves. Sitting in the cool shade of one entrance was a group of women sewing.

Lady Chater introduced me to them, and my eyes and mouth opened widely in amazement as I looked at their incredible work. They were embroidering the most intricate designs on a silk-like material, and I was fascinated.

Unfortunately, I could not speak their language, but I hope the expression on my face indicated how impressed I was. Then, I had the greatest surprise. Lady

Chater asked one of them to measure me, she was ordering an embroidered blouse to give me as a belated 21st birthday gift. I was quite overwhelmed.

A few days later, we returned and there was the blouse—it fitted me perfectly, and the embroidery was so very beautiful. I kept it for years and years. It was difficult to know how to thank those lovely ladies, just sitting there on the rocky floor in the mouth of a cave, producing such exquisite work.

Every day, the blazing sun shone down from a blue sky. On this particular morning, Lady Chater called her chauffeur and we set off in the car, winding our way up into the mountains—from time to time, retreating into sudden blackness as we encountered the tunnels bored through the rocky heights to make travelling possible.

Finally, we reached our destination, a tunnel which had just been completed. The workmen were still there with all the drilling equipment. We left the car and guided by a man carrying a lantern, carefully picked our way along the newly drilled underground passageway.

It was pitch black, apart from the one gleaming shaft of light from his lamp, which pierced the darkness. We seemed to be going on forever, when suddenly, far away, a tiny speck of daylight emerged through the gloom. It grew larger and larger as we drew nearer and nearer to the open air.

Finally, we stepped outside. The view took my breath away, we stood in silent awe and wonder. A sea of misty blue wild hydrangeas spread their way across a vast valley, stretching as far as we could see to the horizon.

Lady Chater quietly said, "No person has ever seen this before, no one has ever been here until today, when they finally broke open the last piece of the tunnel."

What a privilege, it was just like the Garden of Eden. She told me how she was often invited to visit the final opening of a tunnel which—in the majority of cases—displayed undiscovered scenery, and every time she felt overcome by the experience.

We stood there silently, humbled by the magnitude and beauty. It was pure, untouched by human hands, a place of holiness which we treated with reverence—it was beyond words.

Finally, we left, wending our way slowly back through the darkness guided by the one little lantern, what a contrast from a few moments previously. I had been given the most wonderful memory which will remain with me for always.

The weeks went by and suddenly Christmas was almost upon us—it was time to return home. Father's and David's health had much improved and I had enjoyed a wonderful time with some very special experiences.

I felt sad at the thought of leaving the island I had come to love and, especially, Lady Chater. But Father booked up for us to return for a two-week holiday with all the family, the following summer. We had a less eventful journey home and arrived safely on Christmas Eve.

The London Emmanuel Choir

I enjoyed being at Hazelwood Lane and it was good to be back with the children and staff having been away for half a term in Madeira, but I was missing outside interests and friends.

For many years, my mother had taken us to the London Emmanuel Choir Easter and Christmas Festivals at the Central Hall Westminster in London. I loved their singing; it was always a joyous occasion and very popular.

The London Emmanuel Choir was started in 1945 by a husband and wife, Edwin and Muriel Shepherd—always known as Mr and Mrs Shepherd. They gathered together a group of Christians to go and sing anywhere in the country where people had suffered from war damage, and churches and homes had been crushed by the bombing.

They went to sing a Christian message of peace, love and hope—wherever they were invited—to bring comfort to those who had suffered so much loss and sadness. As the years went by, and slowly the country began to recover, there was mention of the choir discontinuing.

But the decision was made for it to carry on and be called the London Emmanuel Choir, (God with Us). It had a maximum of 160 members—there was a waiting list—and was the largest Christian choir in the country at that time.

Every weekend, a part—if not all—of the choir would accept invitations to go and sing anywhere in the country, often staying overnight in the homes of local people.

The only permanent fixtures were the two festivals in the Central Hall Westminster: one at Easter which filled the hall to capacity for two evenings, and one at Christmas which packed the hall to its limit for five evenings.

Initially, Mr Shepherd conducted and Mrs Shepherd accompanied on the piano. In later years, they were joined by an accomplished organist and an outstanding pianist who played together.

Both my consultant and physiotherapist had recommended that I join a choir to help strengthen my lungs. For a long while, I discarded the idea, and then, we went to the Christmas Festival. I looked at all the choir members singing their hearts out to the audience of 2,300 people.

The women were wearing bright velvet capes; the organ was blaring out to its full capacity; the keys of the piano were racing up and down in full splendour; and the singing genuinely made a joyful noise to the Lord. Suddenly, I wanted to be part of this quite unique community.

I wrote to Mr and Mrs Shepherd asking for an interview and explaining that one of my reasons—and only one—was to help with my breathing. A few weeks later, I was invited for a singing test and was accepted. I'm not sure that it was because of the quality of my singing though!

For the first few years, I only went to the comparatively local engagements which did not involve staying away for the night. Even so, these were extremely varied; ranging from small gatherings in tiny chapels to large audiences/ congregations in vast concert halls.

I loved wearing my red cape, as it hid the outline of my brace and, for once, I did not feel different. The highlights were, of course, the Christmas and Easter festivals.

There is something so uplifting about singing to over two thousand people, and even more inspiring when they join in for the communal carols or hymns. I was never tired of doing the same programme five times at Christmas or twice at Easter.

There was, however, one place we visited—which to me was special— Wormwood Scrubs prison. I never lost the feeling of apprehension and exclusion when the huge doors were closed behind us, and the keys rattled in their locks. We sang in the prison chapel—a beautiful place of sanctuary.

It was always full as the choir was very popular and Mrs Shepherd was known as their mother. I found it hard to watch the *lifers* come in—handcuffed to the wardens—if I remember correctly, there were usually about 70 in number. One of them always touched my heart.

He had a lovely cheery smile, his eyes twinkled and he had a long white beard which reached right down to his waist—he looked just like Father Christmas. Every time I saw him—and he always came—I wondered why he was there; where did his *life* go so wrong?

At the end of the service, the prisoners gave us refreshments and we had an opportunity to chat with them, of course, you never referred to the reason for them being in there. Then, it was time to leave and, for me, that was the hardest part.

We went through the doors one by one and they clanged behind us; the echoing sound followed us as we wended our way to the exit. At one point, we crossed an open area and I paused for a moment to look back.

There was a massive wall studded with barred windows, and in between the bars, arms stretched out with hands waving—rows and rows of them, no faces, only arms and hands—bidding us *goodbye*.

Every time I saw this, a lump welled up in my throat. Suddenly, we were out, in the open air, with trees, birds, gardens and the passing traffic. We were *free*.

I was chatting to the prison chaplain following one of our visits. I told him about a group of young people in my church who played several instruments, guitars, flutes etc. and often led the singing. I wondered if he might like them to come to the prison with me one Sunday.

He readily agreed and invited us to be there, three weeks before Christmas. They were so pleased to come with me—if a little apprehensive. Having once again negotiated countless heavy locked doors, we reached the chapel and sat watching the prisoners arriving.

As I looked at the sea of faces in front of me—all men, waiting for the service to start—I could not help feeling nervous. This was very different from singing with the choir with Mrs Shepherd leading.

The chaplain had told me that on the last three Sundays, the prisoners had stamped out the visiting speakers as they expressed their anger at not being able to go home for Christmas. He said not to be disappointed if this happens; just stop quietly, and he will invite us again next year.

The lifers were the last to arrive, once again chained to the keepers, and it was time to begin. The chaplain introduced us and gave us a lovely welcome. I stood up and began by saying how pleased I was to be there.

I told them that I had been there before many times with the London Emmanuel Choir, and Mrs Shepherd sent her love to them and God's blessing. I am sure these words helped to stop any stamping.

Mrs Shepherd had visited the prison for years and years with the choir, and as I mentioned earlier, the inmates looked up to her like a mother.

Everything went well; the singing was good, the young people gave their all, and one of them spoke about his own experience when he was in trouble, and how his faith had meant so much to him. We left, humbled with a memory we would never forget.

Change

In spite of my enjoyment of the choir, and my contentment at school, I began to feel restless. I still thought about the orphaned children in North Africa and wished I could have gone out to work with them; I needed more of a challenge.

One morning the 'Teachers World' a professional newspaper was put through our front door by *mistake*.

I took it up to my bedroom and started to read the advertisements, one immediately caught my eye:

'Wanted, a teacher for infant-aged children and specialising in music. St Mary Magdalene Church School, Liverpool Road, Islington.'

The words stood out. Islington would be a very different place from Palmers Green. I quietly prayed, the more I prayed, the more I felt I should apply for it, and after a few days, I did. I received an invitation to attend for interview.

I travelled to the school by train and then walked the final part of the journey, and what I saw took my breath away; it was so different from the area where I lived and worked. High, dirty, run-down tenement buildings were stacked together alongside old terraced houses with notices on their doors:

'No Dogs, No Irish, No Blacks.'

I approached the school, the building was new, far more modern than Hazelwood Lane, but when I entered and was shown a class of children, I nearly cried. So many were from African and Caribbean backgrounds.

Their little black faces, brown eyes and glorious smiles were a joy. They confirmed why I was there. It was so different from Hazelwood Lane where every single child came from a white indigenous background.

The school catered for children up to the age of 11, there was a junior and infant department. I was interviewed by the headmaster, the deputy head who was also the head of the infant department and the governors.

It seemed to go well and, having seen the multi-racial aspect of the school, I told them how I had wanted to go to Africa. Also, how much I would love to work with children from many different cultures and backgrounds.

There were, however, two concerns: first, they really wanted to appoint someone with an Anglican Church background, and I was a member of a Baptist Church, and secondly, the date of the autumn term when I would be starting, was a week earlier than Hazelwood Lane, and I would still be returning from Canada where I had booked a holiday.

The deputy head, Win Warner, was very concerned about this. I waited for a decision, expecting to be turned down, and finally, the headteacher came out. I was offered the post and, I could hardly believe this, was replacing a Miss Brown who was going to Africa as a missionary!

For several years now, I had enjoyed driving around on my Vespa and relied on it to get to college and school, but I was beginning to think that it was time I had a car. I started saving, and although my father was against women drivers, he helped me buy a small second-hand Fiat.

Due to the current Suez Crisis, there was petrol rationing. Driving lessons and tests were temporarily abolished. Probationers were allowed to drive without any escort. So, I was able to travel freely wherever I wanted, and when, I finally took my test, I passed without any problem.

Canada

My friend Jan had a sister living in Canada. She very much wanted to visit her but was apprehensive about going alone. One evening she asked me if I would be willing to accompany her.

I loved the idea, and we booked two passenger tickets on the Empress of England for the outward journey, and two on the Empress of Britain for the return—both were brand-new liners.

The Empress of England sailed from Liverpool to Montreal. It was a lovely warm summer day as we set off. My father was driving, Jan and me in his car, and also my mother who came to wave us off.

The bustle and excitement at the docks will never be forgotten as we pushed our way through the crowds of passengers and onlookers, eventually, finding our way on board and to our cabin.

We then quickly went to one of the decks where we could see my parents way down below, standing and watching with all the onlookers. Eventually, they saw us. We had been given some long streamers and we threw them in their direction.

Surprisingly, they caught two. Finally, the huge liner's horn sounded—it was deafening—and the little tugs slowly pulled us out of the harbour. The streamers tore in two: one half with my mother and father, and the other half still tightly held in our hands as we waved *goodbye* and the onlookers, gradually, disappeared out of sight.

It was a wonderful voyage of 3105 miles which took 12 days, and then, Jan's sister Rosemary and her family met us in Montreal.

They really looked after us. We explored Montreal, Ottawa and Toronto, and then, stayed for several nights in the Laurentian mountains. There, we slept in tiny log cabins and the chipmunks peeped in the open windows at night. Finally, we spent an amazing day at Niagara Falls.

Here, we sailed in the *Maid of the Mist;* almost touching the vast fall of water from the Horse Shoe Falls on the Canadian side. The sound was deafening as the huge volume of water crashed around us.

The three weeks went unbelievably quickly, not a moment was lost before it was time to return home; this time sailing on the Empress of Britain.

The Empress of Britain was a beautiful liner. Having been built in 1956, she was just a year old when we boarded her and searched for our cabin. We then went to reserve our table for mealtimes.

Unfortunately, the first sitting was full, so, we had to settle for the second—which, as we found out later—was a blessing. Dinner was served and a delightful Canadian girl named Barbara came and sat next to me.

We chatted socially, but she made no mention of her home, family or where she was going when we arrived in England. We had now begun our journey and were slowly making our way along the St Lawrence River; darkness fell, and it was time to retire for the night.

I lay in the little cabin bed, it was very comfortable, but I could not sleep.

Suddenly, it was as if a voice was saying, "Get up and go to the deck above you."

At first, I took no notice—this was ridiculous—was I dreaming? But the words kept repeating themselves in my mind, I felt as if I could hear them and yet they were silent. I sat up. Jan was sound asleep. What should I do? Should I wake her, should I really go up to the deck?

They continued, "Get up and go to the deck above you."

They still continued and finally, I climbed out of bed and strapped my brace over my nightie.

Jan woke up and asked, "Daphne, are you all right, what are you doing?"

"I don't really know," and I tried to explain my feelings.

Pulling a dress over my brace, I fumbled my way along the corridor and up the stairs to the open deck.

There was an eerie silence in one way as no one was about, but the sound of the waves and the ship's engine resonated through the air as the ship ploughed its way through the water. I stood on the deck. The night air felt cool; a breeze fanned my face.

What should I do, where should I go, was this really just a dream? Holding on to anything I could grab, I made my way towards the end of the deck, and then, I saw her. Barbara, the girl who sat next to me at dinner. She was standing high up leaning over the edge.

"Barbara, Barbara," I shouted, "What are you doing? Come here, come down, Barbara."

She turned and looked at me, "Leave me, please, leave me, please, go away."

"I wouldn't."

I went and stood as near to her as I could. I was pleading over and over again for her to come down. It seemed as if she hung on up there for an eternity.

One minute, she was shouting, the next minute, she was crying. Finally, after what seemed like hours and hours—although it was probably only about 20 minutes—she slowly, very slowly and hesitantly, climbed down and flung her arms round me.

Slowly, together we walked to a seat and sat down. The moon was shining, brightly reflecting on the rolling waves and a few remaining distant icebergs far out on the horizon. The slight swell of the water caused a rhythmic rocking which felt comforting—we were at peace.

Barbara told me how she had a broken engagement; she felt her world had come to an end and had deliberately bought just a one-way ticket with the intention of ending her life én route. She had hardly any belongings, and absolutely nowhere to go when she reached England.

Time went by. I felt sad for her and helpless; all I could do was sit there silently listening. Then, I found myself sharing with her my faith in the Lord Jesus and how it had helped me, it was as if the words were taken out of my mouth.

She looked at me and said, "I wish I could have that faith."

"You can."

There, in the light of the moon and the stars, with the water lapping around us, Barbara and I knelt down and she committed her life to Christ. We finally returned to our cabins. It was 4 o'clock in the morning.

I was so thankful that we were at the second sitting for breakfast. Jan and I had just arrived when Barbara came in smiling.

She stood at the end of the table—there were about eight of us there—and looking straight at everyone said, "I've got something to tell you, I became a Christian last night and I'm so happy."

When we finally reached Liverpool, my parents were there to meet us. Knowing Barbara had nowhere to go, I invited her to join us, which she did. My parents were good at welcoming people into our home, and although I didn't give any details, they were happy for her to drive back with us in the car.

Barbara stayed for several weeks and then, went to London Bible College as a residential student. After she had completed a year's course, she returned to Canada and, eventually married.

Her husband became the principal of a large theological college, and Barbara's faith has always remained strong. We are still in contact and recall that very special evening, sailing down the St Lawrence River in the moonlight, so many years ago.

St Mary Magdalene School

It was indeed a new beginning. Due to my Canadian visit, I started at St Mary Magdalene school in Liverpool Road Islington, a week after the term had begun. I was so pleased, I had learnt to drive and could use my *car,* even though I was still waiting to take my test.

When I arrived, everyone had already settled in. The environment and atmosphere were so different from Hazelwood Lane—being a combined Infant and Junior School, I began to wonder if I had made the right decision.

My classroom was bright and airy, surrounded by large glass windows and a patio door—which led directly into the playground. What a contrast from the thick enclosed walls from my previous school, with its rows of dual desks, so unlike the Formica-topped tables facing me now. The children came straggling in through the classroom door.

As soon as they arrived—and no orderly lines or bell ringing—they shouted out, "Morning, Miss," as they passed me by on their way to the cloakroom, then, returned to choose where they wanted to sit.

Finally, it seemed they had all arrived, so I decided, it was time for me to take some sort of control; how I missed Miss Hughes' quiet discipline! I looked at the assortment of cultures, the different coloured complexions, the varied shades and styles of hair, then slowly, went through table by table, asking them about their families and where they lived.

They were very good and listened as each one responded. Then I came to two little boys sitting in the front. There was silence.

A bright-eyed blonde girl in the far corner shouted out, "They don't know what yer saying, they don't speak no English."

Those words hit me, they were so true. How was I ever going to handle this? How could I begin to teach children who could not understand a word I was saying? What was even more important, I could not understand a word they were saying.

The headmaster was kind, but he was much more comfortable with the junior age group having never taught infants, we were just the *little ones*. The Deputy Head Win, gave me some ideas as to how I could occupy these children, but, right from the very beginning, I was deeply concerned about them.

Apart from the two boys, there were others for whom English was their second language and their vocabulary was very limited.

In complete contrast, a number of the indigenous children came from families who had worked—sometimes for several generations—in the nearby Chapel Street Market. They were happy to chat away all day like Linda who had quickly informed me that Petros and Nicholas didn't know what I was saying!

David's gran had worked all her life in the market and one day he came in and gave me an Amaryllis.

"Gran says this is for you."

It was the first time that I had ever seen or heard of this flower, and still today, when I see one I think of David and his gran. The market people were so kind and generous. I learnt to love them dearly.

It was the beginning of October. I had been there for three weeks and was taking the register one morning, when the children suddenly called out, "There is someone outside."

Standing, looking through the patio door, was a little girl of Caribbean origin. It was a cold morning and she stood there shivering; only in a cotton frock, no coat, no socks, no shoes. A boy opened the door and invited her in, but she was very reluctant to move, she was totally alone.

I went out to her, gently took her hand and brought her inside. Then, I asked one of the children to go and fetch our school's welfare helper. The little girl remained silent, only her teeth chattered with the cold. The welfare helper came and took her to the headmaster.

They found a spare coat in the lost property and tried to give her a drink, but she would not take anything, and she would not speak. The local Church Army Sister Jean—who worked closely with the school—was then contacted. Jean arrived and, trying to give her reassurance in every way she possibly could, asked her to take her to where she lived.

At the end of the afternoon, Jean returned and told me she had found the home and asked if I would like to visit it and meet the family. I jumped at the idea and together we walked off down the road. Once again, the notices on the doors just hit me:

'No Irish. No Blacks. No Niggers.'

We turned a corner into a narrow side street flanked by high concrete tenement buildings. Although it was still daylight, it seemed so dark as we mounted the dirty stone steps. We passed the one communal toilet shared by all the apartments and then the kitchen.

Finally, on the fourth floor, we stopped. Children's voices, laughing and talking echoed through a door as Jean knocked. A lovely Jamaican mother turned the latch and fearfully peeped out.

When she saw us, she immediately welcomed us in, and we were surrounded by a cluster of smiling faces all wanting to greet us with warmth and kindness.

"Please, come and sit down," she pulled a blanket off a chair—but it wasn't a chair, it was a packing case. I could not believe my eyes; there was no furniture, only packing cases. Packing cases for beds, packing cases for chairs and a packing case for a table. The little girl—who had come into school—was laughing like all the other children; her name was Precious. I was lost for words.

Although they spoke English, it was difficult to understand their accent, and, of course, it was difficult for them to understand mine.

We began to talk with the mother. They had all come as a family on the Windrush liner which had been transporting families from the Caribbean since 1948 (and incidentally continued to 1971).

They had been told that England needed them and would welcome them, and the streets were made of gold. How totally different it was. The abuse they were receiving was horrific; they had no clothes, no bedding, no toys, little food and even the sun—though it shone brightly—was cold.

Precious had been to school in Jamaica, but that was so different. She was in a class of 50 or 60 children sitting on mounds of earth, learning by rote from a blackboard.

Her mother had sent her to our school as she had been told to, but could not leave the other children to take her. Having shown her the way the day before, she hoped she would have the courage to go in by herself.

That afternoon, I learnt so much in one hour, it was an experience far beyond my imagination. When I returned home later that evening, and told my family, they too had no idea what the conditions were like. There we were, in a beautiful house with everything we needed.

I found it so difficult to absorb and comprehend. I wanted to take things in to help them, but it was not advisable. If I took them for one family, then I would have dozens more asking and expecting gifts as well.

As the days went on, I was so thankful to know that Jean and others—including the market people—provided clothing, furniture, food and toys for the children, and the father found work to do, but the prejudice and abuse continued.

Precious settled in well with a warm coat to wear and socks, as well as shoes. Of course, she was not the only one who arrived like this with her family.

Many others came, bewildered by the reception they received, desperately lonely, deceived and hurt. The situation was still being investigated in 2018, 64 years later.

The longer I worked as a teacher, the more I realised that our job was far wider than the boundaries of education. Some of the houses on the opposite side of the road to the apartment blocks did have washing and toilet facilities, but one of these was used for completely the wrong reason.

The children recently had their school photos taken and were given the prints to take home, the majority returned with the money to buy them.

Peter, aged six, walked in and slammed his down on my desk. "My mum doesn't want mine," he said and walked away.

During the morning break, I asked him to come and talk to me. It was then that I noticed a faint bruise down the side of his face, and I decided to report it. As a result, a social worker went to investigate the situation, and after a lengthy enquiry, it was found that Peter was plunged into an icy cold bath every time he seemingly misbehaved.

There were many other acts of cruelty, and a few months later, he was finally taken into care. What a tremendous responsibility we have when working with little children.

In spite of the deprivation, the longer I worked in this area, the more I loved the wide variety of people in the community. The majority had a great sense of humour, would do anything to help anyone and were nearly always cheerful!

Win

Win was the deputy head teacher of the whole school and was also responsible for the infant department. It consisted of just three classes: Win's, mine and Mary's. We all worked together extremely well.

Mary was married with a family, and she had to leave promptly at the end of the afternoon. It meant that Win and I saw a great deal more of each other as we spent time tidying up and sorting things out together.

Win was a great help to me as I tried to settle down in my new environment. I soon discovered she lived at home with her parents; caring for them as they became less able due to their age. One day, she asked if I would like to go and have a cup of tea with her and meet her parents before setting off on my long journey home.

I was delighted. She lived reasonably near in Highbury and, normally, travelled to school by bus. The Suez Crisis had finally ended, and petrol rationing had ceased. Now that I had passed my driving test, I could happily drive us both to her home.

We parked in the road outside her Victorian terraced house, there was no driveway or garage.

Win opened the front door and a friendly voice called out from the kitchen, "Come in, duck, make yourself at home."

A welcome coal fire glowed in the hearth of the tiny front room, and I sat down in a comfortable armchair. Once again, how different from my home, but oh so friendly. I just relaxed. Win's mother came in with a pot of tea, her white hair twisted around her rosy smiling face, and a large apron covered her dress.

"Have you had a good day?"

That first visit became one of many. It was not long before I took Win home every day, unless she had a meeting with the headteacher, and I nearly always stopped for a cup of tea. I soon learnt the geography of her house.

There was no bathroom or wash basin as such, everyone washed in the kitchen sink. The toilet was outside, so even in the rain, you had to nip out of the kitchen door and disappear as quickly as you could. It was some time before I realised where the bath was!

A large portable zinc tub was kept in the garden shed. It was then brought out when needed and placed in front of the kitchen fire. It was half filled with hot water that was heated in a copper boiler, and then, diluted with cold water from the sink before bathing could begin.

Win's father repaired tyres in a room halfway up the stairs, so the smell of rubber permeated the whole house, but you got used to it. Of course, there was no central heating, and on the occasions when it snowed, the frosted flakes would pile up and penetrate through the gaps in the sash windows.

When the weather was bad, I would stay there for the night. Although I loved it and the welcome was so warm, I was freezing in the bedroom and found it difficult to sleep.

When we were approaching Easter, Win asked me if I would be interested in going to Guernsey with her during the holiday; she then explained why. She was a little older than I am, and after the war, she joined a group of young people who went to help those who had suffered in a particular way.

Win went to Guernsey in the Channel Islands. It had been occupied by the Nazis, and she stayed with Mrs Thompson, a lady whose husband had died and all her livestock had been taken during that time.

Win helped her replace her animals, and she also purchased two cats which they took to cat shows and occasionally won a trophy. Mrs Thompson was now quite independent, but Win liked to visit her occasionally.

We had a glorious holiday in Guernsey. I loved the island as soon as I got off the ferry, and it was a privilege to meet Mrs Thompson. We stayed in a beautiful cottage where the milkman left a posy of freesias on the doorstep with the milk; such a special touch.

I still remember it every time I see freesias, and afterwards, Win and I often gave each other a bunch.

The following Easter we went to Paris and stayed with two ladies who had worked in the French underground movement during the war. Once again, Win had a connection as she did with Mrs Thompson. It was a real privilege to listen to their experiences and the risks they took during the Nazis' occupation.

We continued going on many holidays to Ireland, Austria, Norway and throughout Britain. Once or twice, we joined my family, and on a particular occasion, stayed in the Carbis Bay hotel which quite recently was used for the climate change conference.

When we were there, it was owned by my aunt and uncle. Their cat had recently given birth to a litter of kittens and I returned home with the dearest little grey and white one, whom I named Prudence.

Sadly, she came to an untimely end a few months later when one of the boys accidentally shut her in the door and she had to be put to sleep.

Due to the long travelling distance to and from school, I had to leave the London Emmanuel Choir. It was too much to journey into the centre of London every Wednesday evening for practices, immediately after school. I missed the fellowship and the joy of singing enormously, but I found another interest.

Win was a trustee of what was then the British and Foreign Bible Society, known now as simply the Bible Society. At that time, the headquarters was in London and Win belonged to a group of volunteers who met there once a month on a Saturday. I decided to join them and trained as a guide for the packing department.

Numerous visitors from many different countries came to look around on a Saturday, and it was my responsibility to show them the department where Bibles were parcelled up ready to be sent off. This was fascinating. Bibles were sent all over the world and I never knew what to expect.

So many different languages and addresses. The size and weight of each package were according to how it was going to be met at the other end. If a person or donkey was going to transport it, then the parcel would be small.

If, however, it was going to be a lorry, then, the parcel would be appropriately large. Everyone was an individual and every day was different.

This group of volunteers went away together from time to time for a holiday/conference. On one occasion, we stayed in a hotel with a large veranda overlooking the sea. The proprietor wheeled a beautiful grand piano out onto the veranda for me to play. It was a perfect evening.

The sea was lapping beneath us reflecting the light of a full moon that rose in the sky as darkness fell. I was playing a variety of pieces in the background as everyone enjoyed their drinks and chatter, and, then I started Debussy's 'Claire De Lune'.

Suddenly, all the conversation stopped and all you could hear was the waves lapping on the shore and the piano playing that sensitive piece of music in the moonlight—it was a special moment!

These Bible Society holidays were not just restricted to our group. Local members of the society were also invited, and on this particular occasion, two blind ladies joined us—Jean and Diana. I got to know them very quickly. Diana lived in Cornwall, but Jean came as her friend from London.

When we returned home, Jean travelled with us on the train. In conversation, I asked if she would like to come and stay with me and my family for a few days, and she readily agreed. Jean came a few months later.

As I have said previously, my parents were very good at accepting my various contacts and Jean fitted in extremely well, especially with my father; they had a similar sense of humour. One thing that I will never forget; Jean was in the bathroom washing and she called me. She had dropped the soap on the floor and could not find it. It was so easy for me to go in and see it straightaway; how fortunate I was to have sight.

Another holiday which was organised by the Bible Society was a week at a conference centre in Oosterbeek, Holland. This was specially arranged to break down barriers between Dutch, German and English people of my age, who had experienced the hostility of war.

Although peace had been declared 14 years previously, breaking the barriers and forgiveness was still not easy. It was a precious moment when we all knelt together and shared Holy Communion.

One of the staff, Elsa, desperately wanted to visit England, so, once again, I invited her to come and stay at my home. Elsa stayed with us for several weeks, and then, was accepted on the staff of Lee Abbey, a Christian conference centre where she worked for many years.

Life quietly continued, and then, changes came.

More Changes

Both my brothers were now married. The weddings were happy occasions, but understandably, I was not invited to be a bridesmaid. No one mentioned why, but to me, it was obvious because I could not wear a low-backed dress.

My mother quietly said, "I'm sorry, you haven't been invited."

An aunt loudly protested in the church, "Why are you not a bridesmaid?"

I found it extremely embarrassing. I was not hurt during the actual services and concentrated on caring for my elderly grandmother, but I did find both receptions difficult.

All the family were together at the top table: my brothers were *best man* for each other, my sister was a bridesmaid, and of course, my parents joined them. Only I was sitting with relatives and friends.

With the boys leaving home and my sister going to university, the house seemed empty, but there was one new addition. As requested, my parents gave me a tiny Yorkshire Terrier for my birthday. I called him Scamp. He was a feisty little fellow, a great character and I was very fond of him.

Like my father, I had always loved dogs, and especially, the Airedales we had. Apart from walking them regularly, I would go with him to the vet when they were ill. One of them died from distemper, a deadly disease which thankfully has been virtually eradicated through vaccination.

I continued teaching at St Mary Magdalene for a number of years; enjoying the area and Win's company, and I'm not really sure, why I decided to leave. I think, perhaps, I wanted to once again widen my experience.

I applied for a teaching position in Tottenham, but unfortunately, I was not happy there. The pet rabbit I kept for the children was stolen, and I never felt relaxed.

I had heard about an infant school in Rhodes Avenue, Muswell Hill where they were pioneering *free activity*, and this interested me. The headteacher was very dedicated to this current new approach. I went to see her and was appointed to the staff.

It took me a little while to adapt, but I quickly saw the advantages. Each room was allocated to a subject, there were maths, reading, writing, painting, science and clay modelling rooms. The children could choose where they went, as long as they visited every room each week.

I remember four six-year-olds making a large clay model of the Queen Mary which took three days. It lit up with batteries, and the maths and writing which transpired was outstanding. We had to be extremely well-organised to make the system work, but it was worth it.

Three years went by, and Win was appointed as headteacher of South Haringey Infant School. She needed a new deputy head and the local education officer asked me to apply, and I was offered the post. South Haringey was, in many ways, similar to St Mary Magdalene—the community was very multi-racial.

Within six years, the school population had changed from all the children coming from a totally white English indigenous background, to being completely multicultural, apart from just five of the original families. The building was old but very homely, and it was a happy school to work in.

There was a member of staff who came from South Africa. I shall always remember her because of what she told us and why she came to live in England. She, her husband and one of her boys had pale skin, but her other son had dark skin like his grandfather.

Whenever they had previously gone to the shops or anywhere special as a family, the son with the dark skin had to go alone through a separate door and frequently was forbidden to join his parents and brother. It was so hard to imagine a family being divided in this way and the effect it must have had on the young boy.

One day, when Win was away on a course, a helper called me to watch a little Greek girl walk across the hall. She was swaying from side to side. We asked the mother to take her to the hospital. Sadly Pania had a brain tumour, she died a few weeks later on her sixth birthday.

It was my privilege to attend the funeral in the Greek Orthodox Church. Carrying candles, we slowly filed past the tiny open white coffin. Pania wore her birthday dress, she looked beautiful, lying there so peacefully—but it was so sad.

Sunset

My father inherited the family civil engineering business *Biggs Wall and Company*, from my mother's family. Knowing that my brothers would one day take over, he graciously made provision for my sister and me, by purchasing two attractive homes for us.

Mine was a beautiful bungalow set in the midst of glorious Hertfordshire countryside in the little village of Datchworth. At the time when he bought it, I was still at school. I had a great aunt, Auntie Louise, the sister of my grandfather.

Auntie Louise was an artist and had travelled extensively, spending many years in America. She finally decided to retire but had nowhere to live. My father offered her this bungalow on the understanding that when she no longer needed it, it would be mine. Many years passed, and Auntie was in her 90s.

One afternoon the telephone rang, and my mother called me saying, "Auntie Louise is going to live with a cousin, she feels unable to cope alone in the bungalow any more, that means it is yours."

Suddenly, a new world opened up before me.

We had visited Auntie many times. I loved the garden with a pond and summer house. The views of open countryside stretched away to the horizon, both from the back and the front. I felt free when I went there, but I had always seen it as Auntie's home, now, suddenly overnight, it was mine.

My parents suggested I let it and continue living at home, but I decided to go and look at it, for the first time—alone. I wandered in the garden and there was an elderly gentleman weeding.

He introduced himself as Mr Andrews and told me he had worked for Miss Wall (my auntie) for many years and hoped he would be able to work for me as he loved the garden. The day was coming to its close, and there—facing the bungalow and shedding its radiant, golden light across the fields—was a magnificent sunset.

I stood there silently. This was why Auntie had named the bungalow *Sunset*. I was speechless—it was so beautiful. Late that summer evening, I returned home. I had made up my mind and told my parents I would be leaving home.

It wasn't long before I moved in, taking Scamp with me. I had a basic amount of furniture, my bedroom suite, and a solid circular oak table and four chairs which I purchased with delight and still have today. My parents helped me buy a sofa and armchairs, and my grandmother bought me a complete set of cutlery.

The one thing Auntie Louise left in the bungalow was her lovely Goetze mini grand piano which I treasured for many years. I shall never forget that first night. As I lay in bed, completely alone, the sounds were so different.

No traffic, just an occasional cow mooing in the nearby field. Also, the raucous chorus from the turkeys on the local farm and an occasional, owl's hooting.

My parents were concerned for my safety as I knew no one. But they need not have worried as the village people were so friendly and quickly introduced themselves. They all knew Auntie and I soon learnt what a character she was. She made her own hats and would ride everywhere on her cycle wearing them!

She was a great lover of animals and on more than one occasion, had safely shut a fox in her garage until the hunters had gone. Many of the villagers brought sick animals to her, and wild birds, whom she would painlessly put to sleep, if really necessary.

She played the organ in the little chapel, and was loved and respected by all who knew her. I had a hard reputation to follow.

My next-door neighbour welcomed me with open arms and became one of my greatest friends. Her daughter and grandchildren lived a few cottages down the lane with their husband and father Barry Norman, the famous film critic.

The couple living two doors away, invited me to musical evenings when we sat in their sun lounge, looking across the beautiful countryside and listened silently to recorded classical music—so relaxing.

On the first Sunday, I went to the village church which I could see from my bungalow. It was only a short distance up the lane. The vicar made me very welcome and came to see me the following week. I did not find the formal Matins service easy with my background in Baptist worship.

I knew all the wording by heart from my boarding school days and was determined to *give it a go;* sadly, the little chapel where my aunt had played, had closed down.

However, there was a slight setback. A few weeks later, the vicar came to see me again. Some of the members had complained that I was taking Holy Communion and I had not been confirmed. The vicar himself was happy to give it to me but explained that it would be much easier if I was confirmed. I protested.

I had been baptised by immersion as an adult, surely, that was sufficient to confirm my faith in the Lord Jesus. Do they have a right to prevent me from obeying my Lord's command? For me, it was a dilemma. Should I stop going and travel to the nearest Baptist Church five miles away in Hertford, or be confirmed?

The vicar suggested that I look at confirmation as an entry into the Anglican Church rather than confirming my faith. Finally, I accepted that idea and was confirmed by the Bishop in St Albans Abbey.

Every Sunday, after church, I would drive back home, taking Scamp with me and often collecting my grandmother on the way. Meeting up with the family for lunch was a happy occasion, and a chance to catch up with all the news.

My one difficulty was travelling to Haringey for work. I tried going by train, but driving in the car was easier, it took a good hour, however, I worried about leaving Scamp alone at home for so long.

I was offered a teaching post in the village school, but as I had only been the deputy head at South Haringey for a short while, I decided to continue there for at least another year. As so often happens in life, the situation resolved itself in an amazing way.

Although I no longer took Win home, I saw her at school and once or twice, she came to stay with me. I was very much aware that her parents were becoming increasingly frail, and that year, both of them died. Win decided she would move out of London and she came to stay with me while looking at property in the Hertfordshire area.

We quickly realised how well we got on. I loved her company and she loved the bungalow. We decided to try living together on a more permanent basis. She sold her family home and moved in with her belongings.

It worked extremely well, and in time, Win paid for an extension and the bungalow was registered in both our names. We lived happily together for many years.

I finally stopped praying for the husband I had hoped to meet.

The main difficulty now was both of us travelling to Haringey, and if there was a problem with the traffic or weather and we were delayed, it meant that both the head and deputy were missing. We knew we would have to consider changing our school, but how, or where?

We looked at the local advertisements, and for a while, nothing came up. Then suddenly, we saw two infant headships advertised in Letchworth. Should we apply? We did. One school was completely new, situated on a London overspill housing estate on the outskirts of Letchworth.

The other was right in the centre of the town, in an old original Garden City building. It was a strange arrangement, we both applied for both schools. Win gave me a reference for the schools she was also applying for! To our amazement, we were called up for the interview.

A number of teachers had applied, but we were the only ones who had responded to both! We were interviewed individually by a panel of education officers and governors, and then, asked to wait.

As we sat talking with the other applicants, we realised that we were the only ones from outside, everyone else taught reasonably locally and was employed by Herts County Council. It was a very long day. Finally, the door opened and the chairperson emerged.

We looked up expectantly, and Win and I were called in. I felt I was in a dream as she told us to sit down and said we had both been appointed. Win had the new school on the housing estate and I had the old one called Hillshott in the centre of the town.

I could not believe my ears, and the reality of the situation suddenly hit me. She then asked if it would be possible for Win to release me at Easter, as my school had been without a headteacher for some time. Win's school would not be completed until July, so she was not needed until then.

So, Win agreed! It also helped from the Haringey point of view as the head and deputy would not both be leaving together. It was bad enough that they were both going within a few months of each other.

We left in a daze and decided to go and buy something special for tea to celebrate. Having bought a few treats we drove off, but could not understand why people kept shouting and several cars hooted, they couldn't know our news.

Finally, we stopped. Win got out and noticed that we had left all our shopping on the car roof!

Hillshott School

The road leading to Hillshott, with the same name, was bedecked with flowering pink blossom trees. I paused at the gate and stood looking at the strange, gaunt building ahead of me. It did not look like a school, let alone an infant school. I crossed the playground, climbed the front steps, and entered the double doors.

Almost immediately, I was standing in the main hall. I could hardly believe my eyes. The extensive staggered, pink oak floor shone with polish. A huge Edwardian stage with heavily weighted dark green velvet curtains dominated the far end.

A tiered gallery, stretched above my head, accessed by a spiral staircase. The acting headteacher Dorothy Cutler came to welcome me and explained that the school was originally built as the community centre for Letchworth Garden City.

The hall was the theatre and Laurence Olivier, Flora Robson and the D'Oyly Carte Opera had all performed on the stage in its early days. The centre had to close during the war and, afterwards, was bought by the Hertfordshire Education Authority.

A corridor with classrooms had been added, but the main part of the building remained unchanged. As I was shown around, I noticed the hand-blown glass in the doors and the paying-in counter by the main door.

The original grand piano was still standing in the lower classroom and the *dressing room*, which I later turned into the staff room, had an inglenook fireplace.

The rooms were varied in size, some were small, and a very large one was reached by two flights of stairs; this was used for team teaching with 60 children. What a fascinating and exciting place to work in.

Dorothy Cutler was a retired headteacher, very experienced, with a caring and gentle personality. In the years ahead, she was always there to help, advise and encourage me—a professional colleague and a true friend. We walked around the school together, and she introduced me to all the staff and of course, the children.

The staff seemed very friendly, but the thing that impressed me the most was the children from different nationalities. The majority came from the Punjab and the Caribbean, but there were others from different parts of the world.

At my interview, it was mentioned that the school was multicultural, but I had not appreciated how multicultural, schools like this were linked with London, but not Hertfordshire.

I soon learnt that Letchworth Garden City, being a Quaker town, had welcomed immigrant families, and provided housing for them.

Hillshott, being in the centre of the town—where the original housing was—had, therefore, received many of these children into the school. I also learnt that we were known as the *black school* and were not very popular with some of the local public.

As far as I was concerned, this was exactly the challenge and work I would love. I was absolutely delighted and longing to start.

I settled into the school quickly and enjoyed the general activities and responsibilities of a headteacher: getting to really know the children individually, meeting the parents, organising the curriculum, unravelling day-to-day problems and also making time to teach, music being my speciality.

Morning assemblies were open to anyone who would enjoy coming, the hall was so large there was plenty of room for visitors!

I had only been in the school for a few months when I received an unbelievable shock at a governors' meeting. The County Education officer attended and this was unusual. He told us that it had been decided to build a new junior school on a different site.

The present junior school was old and run-down, unlike Hillshott, it was an outdated school building which definitely needed replacing. The officer then continued: "We shall then build a new infant school adjoining it."

I think my heart stopped beating, build a new infant school, replace our beautiful traditional *community theatre* with a square brick object—surely not.

I immediately protested and was told, "That is the plan."

The months went by and the new junior school was almost complete. I had numerous meetings with the governors and parents, and we all protested against the idea. Then suddenly, a very unexpected event changed the plans. The Pix

Brook had been diverted to avoid the new building, and it had consequently caused flooding lower downstream.

It was then realised that a further diversion needed for a second building would cause further major problems. After much consideration, it was finally decided by the authority to keep our building and—even though it was listed—undertake alterations to modernise it, so it complied with current regulations. We rejoiced!

The next two years were a little chaotic as builders moved in, but the staff and governors were asked for advice and suggestions which were always considered. When this happened, I appreciated that, although the school had been functioning since 1946, it had never been adapted.

The builders needed to do some work under the stage and they had to clear out mattresses, beds and even unused Elsan toilets left from the time it was used as a public air raid shelter during the war.

A second spiral staircase was installed at the far end of the gallery, so that it could be used as a library, and a nursery was built at the end of the long corridor, which enabled me to admit four-year-old children. Sinks were put in all the classrooms and the whole building was sensitively upgraded.

When the work was finally completed, we began to have visitors to see it. For many years, architects from this country and abroad (a number from Japan), came to see the unusual historic design, relating to both the first Garden City and a modern school.

We held a number of special occasions to which the local community was invited, Maypole dancing, the distribution of harvest gifts and, of course, Christmas. What a joy it was for me to produce the nativity play each year with nearly two hundred children on that magnificent, historic stage. They became a tradition with special guests sitting in the gallery!

We were one of the first schools in the country to celebrate Diwali, the Sikh Festival of Light in November that paved the way for Christmas. A close relationship with the Sikh community developed, and I counted it a privilege when they invited me to speak at the opening of their new Gurdwara.

One concern I had was the lack of provision for children who could not speak English, and their own mother tongue also was not fully developed and needed enrichment. So, often, they sat for hours not understanding what was being said.

For children of infant school age, this could be very hard, especially, if they had recently arrived from another country and were feeling lost and confused. At that time, no additional staff were provided by the education authority for these children.

So, I decided to personally appoint a teacher and an assistant. There was a little room attached to the hall which was not large enough for a classroom. We equipped it with cooking materials, toys, creative art equipment, and books.

The children who could not speak English were withdrawn here in small groups—and as far as possible, selected to be with those who spoke the same language—they would then enjoy the activities chatting with each other.

The Teaching Assistant, Madhu, was a refugee from Uganda and, partly because of this, related to the children so well even if she came from a different part of the world.

I also invited bilingual pupils from the local secondary school who spoke the relevant languages, to come and share stories and poetry in their mother tongue; thus, encouraging the enrichment of the children's first language development which is so important at that age.

The small group also gave the children confidence to try and speak a little English, and the teacher would introduce a few new words. The main purpose was to create a happy relaxed atmosphere where the children could develop their verbal skills.

The staff, and then the inspectors who came in, were initially concerned that by withdrawing these children, I would be accused of racism, but they were willing to let me give it a try and, it worked.

Both the parents of the children concerned and the parents of English-speaking children were happy about the arrangement. Further details of this can be found in my book 'Mother Tongue to English'.

One morning, I received a telephone call telling me that Sir Keith Joseph the government officer for education was visiting Hertfordshire and they would like him to see my school. It was a privilege to be asked, especially, as he had never been in a complete infant school since his appointment, five years previously.

The day came, I had to be in school at 7:30 when the building was surrounded and searched by detectives. Sir Keith arrived and showed great interest in our multicultural work.

He had a *cup of tea* in the home corner of the reception class—much to the delight of the children—and spent some considerable time in each classroom. Afterwards, he had a long conversation with me and spoke highly of the work all the staff were doing which was such an encouragement.

One morning, Madhu came to me and said, how concerned she was about some of the immigrant mothers. They had apparently been kept indoors since arriving in England. We decided to organise evening sessions for them in the same little room as the groups.

Madhu visited as many homes as she could and, explained to the mothers what we were planning to do. She promised them that no man would be present. On the first evening, 12 ladies arrived, and I had to ensure that the caretaker was nowhere around!

They cooked some of their recipes and Madhu communicated with them in the best way she could, as she spoke a little of their various languages.

One mother told her that she had not gone to the toilet properly for weeks but was unable to go to the doctor as she would not be able to make herself understood; she was also worried, in case, she had to see a man.

Madhu offered to make an appointment and go with her, which she did. The mother had serious problems which thankfully were finally resolved. Those groups continued for years.

They grew in number, and when a new family moved into the area, the ladies would immediately invite the mother to join them—often the only place where she would go after her arrival.

After I had been at the school for a number of years, the inspectorate seconded me to do some research on the language development of children who had entered school aged five to seven, unable to speak English, and were left to pick it up without help.

I was based at the Cambridge Institute of Education under the direction of Dr Margaret Peters, an authority on teaching language and reading and had written several books on these subjects. I observed two boys from Bangladesh and one from the Caribbean. It was a fascinating time, but I was pleased to return to Hillshott after a year.

Both Margaret and the inspectorate asked me to write a book on the study and my work. But once back at school, I was immersed with the children and I found it hard to imagine writing anything to be published. Six months later an inspector came into the school.

"How are you getting on with your book?" he asked.

I smiled and remained silent.

He then handed me a notebook and pen, and said, "Start tonight."

I did and, eventually, my book 'Mother Tongue to English' was published by the Cambridge University Press. I was then invited to lecture in schools and universities which was an interesting experience. On one occasion, I attended a conference held in Birmingham.

I only went for one day because it was at the beginning of September, and we were admitting our new children into school—which was far more important to me. I was in the dinner queue when someone came up and enquired as to whether I was Daphne Brown!

I was then asked if I would say a few words about my book and school at the afternoon session. I shall never forget standing on that huge platform facing a massive audience of many cultures, and not having anything prepared.

Quietly, I took a flower out of the arrangement on the stage and, for a moment, held it silently in the air, and everyone waited. (Even in this situation I was still an infant teacher!)

"Look at this beautiful flower, let us imagine, we are showing it to a young English-speaking child. Look at its petals, pink, rose and purple. They are soft like velvet. Look at the leaves, different shades of green, pointed and shining. Let us touch them gently."

"But what do we say to a child who cannot speak English, just, This is a flower."

And so, I introduced my passionate concern for all these young immigrant children who were missing out on the richness of language at such a crucial age in their development. I was on that platform for nearly two hours answering questions!

Dr Margaret Peters—who taught me so much during my year at the Cambridge Institute—was a very special person and a great encouragement when I was writing my book. She was also a tremendous help to my young godchild Jonathan who was having difficulties learning to read.

Following my year studying under her, she frequently visited my school accompanied by a variety of students. Margaret was a devout Quaker and appreciated watching the children as they quietly entered the hall and silently listened to music.

The first time she came, I played a recording of 'The Dance of the Blessed Spirits' by Gluck; she never forgot it, and it became a regular theme tune for her visits!

Letchworth was built by the Quakers, and on several occasions, I attended a gathering at the local Howgills Friends meeting house, to which one of my teaching staff belonged. Margaret became a great friend, and on several occasions, she invited Win and me to stay in her beautiful holiday home in St Mawes, Cornwall.

I greatly missed her loving care, wisdom and advice when she died, and will never forget her funeral service which I was privileged to attend. Although Quaker meetings are usually silent apart from when individual members feel led to speak, Margaret especially asked that 'The Dance of the Blessed Spirits' be played at her funeral.

There were no large wreaths of flowers, everyone brought little vases or jars full of wildflowers which were placed in every corner of the room. All the window sills, tables and coffin was covered with the most beautiful tiny delicate wildflowers.

I opened the post one morning and could hardly believe what I was reading. Hillshott had been presented with a Schools Curriculum Award. This was a special countrywide recognition of schools obtaining a high standard of education. The awards were given every three years, and ours was between 1985 and 1987.

It was a great privilege to go to the Barbican Centre with two of our children and receive a certificate from Professor Charles Handy. On previous occasions, Princess Anne had presented the certificates, but unfortunately, she was unable to attend our particular ceremony.

We were then invited to choose a gift for the school from a selection of samples which were displayed in the theatre entrance. There were a number of pictures, but we chose the most beautiful life-size sculpture of a fox. He duly arrived at Hillshott a few weeks later, and was given a place of honour in the school hall.

Hillshott School Special Memories

Every day at Hillshott was varied, and I woke each morning wondering what to expect, but there were a few experiences which I shall never forget.

Lucy and Polly were twins. Their parents came to see me and explained that Lucy had a severe heart condition and would probably only live until she was five years old. It was so important for her to attend a nursery where she would be really happy for possibly the last year of her life.

Lucy joined us with her sister a few weeks later. She was a delightful little girl, full of fun and socialised so well. It was sometimes hard to watch her, knowing what the future held.

Just before her fifth birthday, Brampton Hospital contacted her parents. They were considering giving Lucy a new, pioneering form of surgery. It was very risky, but it was the only possibility of keeping her alive. The parents agreed.

The day came. We said *goodbye* to Lucy who was as cheery as ever when she left. It was a difficult moment, mixed with both hope and sadness. What I didn't know until the following day, was that a group of mothers from the school held a prayer vigil for her all night, Sikhs, Moslems, Hindus, and Christians.

Lucy made an amazing recovery. The consultant wrote to me saying that he felt the support of the nursery, and school had helped in her recuperation. She returned to Hillshott a few months later. The only thing we had to be careful of was that she did not get overtired.

I had a little chair in my room, it was called Lucy's chair, and whenever she felt tired, she came and sat in it quietly. We had this arrangement throughout all her time with us. Lucy never wasted an opportunity, because whenever there was something she didn't like doing, she would say she felt tired and come and sit in my room on her chair!

I kept in contact with Lucy throughout her junior schooling, but when she went to secondary school, I lost touch. I knew, she was planning to be a social worker. We did meet again many years later.

This concerns another Lucie and her brother Mark. Lucie was the older of the two. She was in the school and Mark was in the nursery; they were both doing well and were part of a very supportive family. Mark then moved into the reception class at the age of five.

One day, his teacher came to me and said she was concerned about his eyesight. In those days, we had glass milk bottles with foil tops in which you made a hole to put the straw. But it seemed that Mark was unable to see the hole.

I suggested to his mother that she take him to an optician, which she did, and they referred him to Moorfields. The phone rang in my office. It was Moorfields. They told me that Mark unfortunately had Batten disease and, would probably, go blind within the next six months.

He and his mother were on their way home and were planning to come in and see me. It was hard waiting for their arrival, and impossible to describe how we felt. All I could do was to assure her that Mark could stay at Hillshott and we would do everything we could to help.

Marks's sight quickly deteriorated, and it was not long before he was unable to see. At first, the authority wanted him to go to a special school, but they finally agreed that he could stay with us.

We appointed a helper for him and put ropes around the school so that he could feel his way, although this was not easy because of all the stairs and different rooms. I learnt Braille with him and he coped extraordinarily well. It was as if he had suddenly been given a sixth sense.

Mark stayed with us until he was seven. He then went to a residential school, and we missed him. He did very well there, particularly, when playing in a band. I visited him several times with his parents. He died when he was 23. His mother kept in contact with me.

Lucie married but tragically died of cancer at the age of 36 leaving three children, who her mother cared for. It is incredible what some people have to cope with.

Every birthday and Christmas, I receive a card and a detailed letter from her with all the news; this has continued for nearly 50 years now, and I so appreciate it.

Many of the teenage girls in the area, particularly those from the Punjab, had arranged marriages. These often worked well; the parents having given thought and care as to whom they chose.

The girls were brought over from their home country to live here with their in-laws, whom they had never met—this was not always easy.

They often said to me, "If you had an arranged marriage you wouldn't have been left on the shelf!"

However, occasionally, things went wrong and the girls came for help. One arrived in my room with burn marks on her fingers. Her mother-in-law had pressed them with a hot iron. I was able to refer her to the Immigrant Safety Centre, which—if my memory serves me correctly—was in Luton; but I am not sure.

Another day, two girls arrived. They told me they were concerned because there was a lady who was shut in a garage and she had not been seen for some time. Madhu and I went to the house, and bypassing the front door went straight to the garage.

There we found a lady lying on the concrete floor under a blanket, and a plate of half-eaten food was on the ground beside her she looked lost, very afraid, and remained silent. We reported it to the social services and later learnt that she had come over as part of an arranged marriage.

It was then discovered that she could not have children, so the family had hidden her in the garage, thus enabling the husband to marry another woman. She was taken to a care home and supported by social services. But, as they said to me, it was difficult to know what to do with someone in this position, especially, as they could not speak any English.

Tragically one of the houses at the back of the school caught fire and, although most of the family were rescued, the mother died. A large funeral was planned, but one morning there was a knock at my office door.

A gentleman came. "Please, can you help us? We have many relations coming over from the Punjab for the funeral, but one of them has been stopped at the airport because there was something wrong with his papers and passport."

"They need someone who was born in England and with a British passport to go and vouch for him and ensure that he returns home after a month."

I set off for Heathrow and on arrival, I was taken into a large hall with benches alongside the walls. Sitting on them, disconsolate and bewildered, were—what looked like to me—a hundred or more people of many races, all being detained for one reason or another.

They were virtually silent and their facial expressions looked confused and lost. I was taken to the person I had come for, of course, I did not know what he looked like.

After showing the various documents I had brought: my bank statement, my electricity bill and, most important of all, my passport, I was told that he could leave with me, providing I vouched for his whereabouts and ensured he left after a month.

This I did, and we returned to Letchworth together, After the funeral and a short stay with the family, he safely went back to the Punjab.

We received a new admission to the top class. The little boy had been adopted and the new parents were so delighted to bring him to the school. He was welcomed by the children and settled in well. A few months later, his adopted mother suddenly died. Everyone was deeply shocked and saddened.

The teacher came to me as she was finding it difficult trying to answer all the children's questions, so, I went up to the classroom. As I sat facing the children—who were sitting on the floor—they looked at me with bewildered eyes as if to say: please, tell us what has happened to Michael's mother, why did she die.

I began to say how sad it was, when a small boy—sitting almost at my feet—suddenly said, "I know what happens when people die. Their dead bodies go in the ground, but their breath flies away and still lives on."

He may have been told this, but those words resolved the children's queries and have remained with me ever since.

A father arrived with his daughter, they had recently moved into the area and wanted her to join us. My secretary took the details of their address, and then, he asked to speak to me. He explained that he was divorced and when his daughter went to stay with her mother, the new partner had sexually abused her.

He asked us not to pass their address on if anyone outside the school asked for it. Donna settled in well. The next-door neighbour brought her to school with her little boy every morning and helped the father to care for her in a number of ways.

Then, one morning, she came in and told me that the father had gone into custody for shooting the mother's partner and she was caring for Donna. I learnt that, although he may have wanted to kill him, he shot the man in the shoulder which did not cause serious harm.

The case was coming up at the Old Bailey, and the day arrived. I was taking assembly when my secretary came in which was unusual.

"I've got someone from the Old Bailey on the phone, they want you to be there by this afternoon, if possible, and act as a witness."

I was somewhat overcome, but I agreed. Having asked my chairman of governors to come with me, we set off together. On arrival, I was told that Donna's father had been acquitted of murder and was not going to be imprisoned for his shooting episode, but they needed to ensure that he was suitable and able to legally care for Donna.

At about 2 o'clock, I was ushered into the courtroom, led to the witness box and made the appropriate oath on the Bible. I found it hard to see Donna's father handcuffed in the dock.

The judge asked me if the father had shown an interest in his daughter's work at school, to which I replied that he frequently came in to hear her read and spent a great deal of time looking at her work.

The judge replied, "Are you aware that he can neither read nor write?"

My heart sank, what a beginning! However, the questioning continued for what seemed like hours, and finally, I left the court and returned to the waiting room. There my chairman of governors was anxiously wondering what was going on.

It was not too long before I was called back for the verdict. Donna's father was going to be released and have the care of his daughter. I watched the handcuffs being removed, and then, I left.

The following morning there was a knock at my door; it was Donna's father. He gave me a beautiful little white Bible as a gift. A few months later, he married the neighbour and, well, they lived happily ever after!

Hillshott and the Royal Family

The children always loved writing to the Queen, and they were so excited when they received a reply, even though it had been written by a *lady in waiting* or a secretary! The envelope arriving with the royal emblem was special, and every letter received a response.

We held a party for the older members of the local community to celebrate the wedding of Princess Diana. The children entertained them with songs and dances.

When the Queen came to open the new leisure centre, we all lined the street, and as she slowly walked by one of our children—as requested by the education officer—presented her with a posy of flowers.

One morning, during the silver jubilee year, the postman rang the bell of my front door exceptionally loudly. I opened it and he handed me a letter; the envelope had a royal emblem. To my astonishment, it was an invitation to a special garden party at Buckingham Palace for people who had worked to enhance relationships with ethnic minorities.

I was utterly confused as to who had organised this, but later, learnt that it was one of the local school inspectors. I asked if Win could go with me rather than my going alone, but was told only husbands, wives or oldest daughters were allowed to accompany those who had been invited.

The day came. I first went to the hairdressers—so did not arrive at the school until 10 o'clock—and I could hardly believe my eyes. The building and all the railings were decorated with bunting, the staff had worked so hard.

After a brief assembly, I walked out of the front door and was amazed to see the playground full of parents and friends from the local community, and they were also lining the streets.

My father had organised a chauffeur-driven car, and my mother came to see me drive off. Slowly, the car went through the gates with everyone cheering and clapping, and we were on our way.

We drove along the Mall, where there were speakers on all the trees to relay messages to the drivers, then, slowly went through the palace gates after showing my invitation to the person on duty, I then left it on the back car seat for safety.

A soldier wearing his bearskin opened the door for me and directed me through the palace, and down the steps to the garden. There I joined the crowd waiting for the Queen. I was early, but it was interesting to watch the people arrive, many in their national costumes.

Finally, the Queen, Prince Philip, the Queen Mother, Prince Charles and Princess Anne came down the steps and joined us. Slowly, they walked around greeting us as we stood surrounding the enormous lawn.

One or two people were called out from the crowd by the attendants to speak to the Queen, and then, to my amazement, they called me. She shook my hand and asked me what work I was doing. The Queen Mother asked me where my school was.

The Queen then thanked me for coming, which to me was unbelievable, but I imagine it was politely indicating that our conversation had finished! I returned to join the crowd.

After the royal family had returned to the palace, the crowd disintegrated. I went for a long walk around the grounds, admiring the roses and standing for some time by the lake with the red flamingos. This was a privilege, as in those days, the palace was not open to the general public.

I returned to the marquee where tea was served with scones and strawberries. The Queen came and joined us. My table was so near, that I got tired of watching her! Eventually, she left and people began to go. I waited, wandering around the gardens for as long as I could.

Finally, I joined the queue to leave. My name was announced so that my driver could hear it through the loudspeakers as he waited in the Mall; then, he drove in and collected me.

We had not been going very far when he said, "So you managed to get in all right."

I couldn't understand why he was saying this, he then continued, "You left your invitation on the back seat, so, I went back and handed it to the man at the gate."

I could not believe what he was saying. "That was my keepsake for this special occasion," I said. "I didn't need it, please turn round and see if I can get it back."

We did, and explaining why we had returned, the keeper at the gate let us through. While they looked for it, I was invited to wait in a room in the palace. I sat on a beautiful red sofa admiring all the many clocks. They found the invitation and we finally drove back to the school where I had left my own car.

The Asian mothers were having their meeting with Madhu. I went in, and told them a little about the day, reminding them that it was because of them and their children that I had this special experience. Eventually, I reached home.

Life at Datchworth

Win and I worked extremely well together; she mainly did the cooking and I worked in the garden. The village of Datchworth—with its surrounding fields and woods—was a beautiful place to live, and we enjoyed many walks with the dogs.

We both joined the village church and I also played the organ for the monthly services in Knebworth Park's little chapel. Because of this, I regularly met Lady Hermione Cobbold and felt that I knew her quite well.

One day, Win came home and said she had admitted a five-year-old girl in her school who had been removed from her home and parents due to neglect. Win was concerned for her welfare as she was consistently bullied. Eventually, the social services moved her to a Children's Home in another district.

Win and I visited her regularly, and after careful thought and discussion with the staff, we agreed for Heather to come and stay with us. I really enjoyed her company as we walked and played together, while Win did the cooking.

This arrangement had continued for over five years when the social services asked me if I would like to legally adopt Heather. I said *no* because I felt she needed a father figure, and so, she went to another family. But we still keep in touch even after 50 years.

One of the boys at the Children's Home had no family connections or relations. He counted the royal family as his family and the walls of his room were plastered with photographs of the Queen, Prince Philip and their children.

We had just celebrated Princess Diana's wedding which Lady Hermione had attended. I told Anthony that I knew someone who had been there as a guest and his eyes opened wide with wonder.

He started to ask me questions, but of course, I could not answer them. When I next saw Lady Hermione, I told her about Anthony.

Straightway she replied, "Invite him to come and have tea with me, so I can tell him all about it."

The following Thursday, one of her chauffeur-driven cars went to the children's home and collected him. He spent the whole afternoon with her in Knebworth House. She never forgot Anthony, and whenever she travelled, she would send him a postcard.

My nephew, Adrian, Gordon's son, came to live with us for a while when he was six years old. I loved taking him across the fields and into the woods. There we particularly enjoyed watching the birds, a reflection of the days when I too was his age on evacuation. Adrian also came to my school.

He was so good at calling me Auntie until we reached the school gate. And then, *Miss Brown* as soon as we walked into the playground. I had to get special permission from the education officer to have him in the school as I was the head, but she graciously agreed.

In time, his stepbrother joined him. I had them both in my nativity play and, now, in their 50s, they still laugh at the photos.

It was a summer evening. By that time, I had been wearing my spinal brace for over 30 years. Win suddenly said, "Why don't we see if you can walk without your brace? You manage to stand when you have taken it off at night time."

For a moment, I could not grasp what she was saying. It was so unexpected and such a surprise, but finally, with her help, I agreed. Evening after evening, Win would practise with me, holding both my hands as she slowly walked backwards and I walked forward with her.

We continued this for days and days, weeks and weeks, months and months. Gradually and slowly, my muscles strengthened and I started to walk upright without flopping forward. At first, it was only for a few minutes, but then, it increased to hours.

Finally, one evening, I wrapped my brace in newspaper and pushed it into our metal dustbin. It was too tall for the lid to go on, but the dustman took it away the following day. I was tired and weak, but I was free. I could never find words to thank Win for her timeless patience.

Win and I both loved dogs. My little Scamp had a sad ending. Win was out walking one day with him and two loose local greyhounds attacked him as if he was a rabbit He lived, but had to spend a week at the vet's under a sunlamp to try and restore his torn fur and mauled body.

After this, he hated being left, so I took him to school with me in the car and he felt safe staying in the back seat. It was May, and in the morning the rain poured down so I had to keep the windows closed. At lunchtime, I asked one of my staff to check on him.

The rain had stopped and the sun was shining, but unfortunately, she did not open any of the windows. When I left at the end of the afternoon, he was dead due to the suffocating heat. I was devastated and whenever I see a dog shut in a car, I try and find the owner.

We decided to go to the Wood Green Animal Shelter and choose another dog. In those days, the shelter was just a collection of huts and a large pen, very different from the large organised and well-known home it is today at Godmanchester. I chose a Welsh Border collie.

Win chose a scruffy little black dog hiding nervously behind a sack. The lady who ran the home advised us not to take her as she was extremely nervous and very defensive. However, Win felt sorry for her and she came home with us.

I called mine Chef as he had a white apron front, and Win called hers Topsy. We had tremendous fun with those dogs. Apart from one holiday in Norway, we always chose places in the British Isles which took dogs and they came with us.

It was true, that Topsy was a handful to control with her barking and incline to bite, but she was loved and slowly improved.

For a while, we worshipped in the Knebworth church just down the lane. It had a grand piano which I played along with the organist for the hymns. After the service coffee was served.

One Sunday, as I was packing up my music, Win came to me and said, "There is someone outside, I think you would like to meet, he has just had coffee."

She knew my love of interesting people. I went outside, and there was an old man who looked like a tramp.

I said, "Hello," and then asked him his name.

He looked at me and replied, "No one has asked me my name for years, it's Bill."

Bill came regularly for coffee, and I always enjoyed chatting with him and asking him where he had been during the week. Sometimes, he would disappear for a while and walk anywhere from John O'Groats to Land's End, and then, he returned.

With his permission, we decided to buy him some new clothes. At first, he was adamant that he wouldn't have them, but finally, he agreed and told me what size he took, including shoes.

The following Sunday, Bill was sitting outside at the back of the church. I gave him the clothes. He said nothing but began to take his old worn-out shoes off with difficulty. Much to my surprise, he let me help. We tugged and pulled, and finally, they came off, but the inner soles were stuck to his feet.

One of the church members was standing nearby, I called out to her, "Please, can you ask Win to bring me a bowl of warm water, she is helping in the kitchen."

I looked at Bill's feet. With all my imagination, I could not have visualised the condition they were in.

As we waited for the water, Bill said, "The only time I've ever pinched anything was when I saw some shoes on a stand outside a shoe shop. My shoes had completely worn out, so I quickly pinched two of those, but when I went to put them on they were two left feet!"

Win brought a bowl of water out wondering what it was for. Like me, she was stunned when she saw his poor feet with the soles stuck to them.

After careful soaking, the soles were removed, the feet were washed and dried; the warm, comfy socks and shoes fitted well. Bill walked away, carrying the bundle of new clothes to a place where he could change. He never said a word, but his silence spoke volumes.

As we thought about Bill, Win and I began to feel guilty. We go to church and then return home to a delicious Sunday lunch, what did Bill eat? I asked him one day.

"I'm not going to tell a lady like you," he replied.

"Why not?"

"'Cos it's not nice."

Finally, he admitted, "I go around and see what I can find in dustbins, of course. What else can I do?"

"Would you like to come home and have lunch with us?"

"No, 'course not, you wouldn't want me in your house."

Bill may be a *man of the road*, but somehow, he managed to be immaculately clean. A few weeks later, obviously, after much thought, Bill agreed to come. The dogs greeted him with joyous barks and he sat, quietly in the lounge fondling them while we prepared the food in the kitchen.

We served lunch as we always did with visitors, putting the vegetables in separate dishes so that each person could take what they wanted. Bill was a little hesitant, but he coped and ate well.

He told us he had been on the road for 40 years, and this was the first proper meal he had. He was happy to come every Sunday when he was in the area, and we were happy to have him, especially the dogs.

After several weeks, he announced that he was going to wash up for us. We were a little taken aback, but, knowing how clean his hands were, (he was constantly in the bathroom washing them), we agreed. We sat relaxing in the adjoining room.

It was an unusual experience, as Bill talked to himself all the time. We listened to him muttering away with the running taps and click of crockery.

Finally, he came out and said he had finished and was off. Then, I went into the kitchen. The door led into the garden and all the windows were wide open, and the crockery and cutlery strewn everywhere wherever there was a space.

"Bill, there are the tea cloths to dry everything."

"No," he retorted. "They're unhealthy, they just collect dirt, you don't want them, the fresh air will dry them. Goodbye."

His words struck me, in a way, he was right. Bill always washed up and after that, left the windows and doors wide open to let the fresh air dry everything, even when it was bitterly cold and there was thick snow on the ground. To this day, I rarely use a tea towel!

The years went by as we both worked in our respective schools. We enjoyed our holidays with the dogs but noticed they were getting older. On this particular year, we went to Devon and sat relaxing on the sand while the dogs played around together. Suddenly, Topsy started to choke and cough.

We could not see anything in her mouth, but we were concerned. As it so happened, a vet van was parked nearby. The person in charge suggested that we take Topsy down to the surgery.

The vet there said he would investigate and find out what was happening, and we would need to leave her with him for an hour.

We sat on the beach waiting, and I remember Win saying, "Do you think she will be all right? I do hope so."

I replied with confidence, "I'm sure, she will."

After an hour we returned. The vet came out, and there was no Topsy.

"It was a piece of seaweed that was causing the problem in her throat, I managed to get it out, but unfortunately, she didn't come round from the anaesthetic," he said.

"Do you mean to say she is dead?"

"I'm afraid so."

We were stunned. We had to leave without her and returned to our cottage in a dream. The holiday was immediately cut short and we left for home the next day.

A few weeks later, we decided to go back to the Wood Green Animal Shelter and choose another dog, hopefully, one that would relate well to Chef who was missing Topsy as much as we were. We went into the large pen where dogs were running loose and a little dog with short brown hair came straight to us.

She was very plain and reminded me of the stray dogs you see wandering in the streets of India. Her name was, apparently, Sally and she was about three years old.

Our efforts to talk to the other dogs were difficult as she would not leave us, and finally, we agreed to have her. On returning home, Chef and Sally immediately played with each other, and all seemed to be well.

That evening Win said, "I'm sorry, but I really don't like her. She's got long monkey paws and she's nothing like Topsy," which was true. Seeing Win was so disappointed, we reluctantly agreed to consider returning her to the home. The following morning was Sunday and as usual we went to church. Chef and Sally were quite happy to be left together. I could hardly believe what I saw when we returned home.

Sally had dragged one of Win's large slippers from the bedroom and put it in her basket in the sitting room.

Win saw it and her eyes filled with tears. "Little Sally, you're staying with us."

She was one of the most affectionate and loving dogs I have ever had, and a great companion through difficult times. She and Chef enjoyed several years together until he was peacefully put to sleep due to old age.

Goodbye

Win retired from her school and trained to join the chaplaincy team at the QE2 hospital in Welwyn Garden City. After working there for a number of years, she became ill and unfortunately, it was cancer.

There had been a delay in the diagnosis as, at that time, scanning equipment in Hertfordshire was very limited, and she had to wait for a vacancy in Bedfordshire. Although it was recommended that she went to a London hospital, she chose to go to the place where she worked and underwent surgery at Easter.

It appeared to be successful, and we booked a holiday in the Scilly Isles for August. But, at the end of July, she was unwell again. Further surgery had problems and failed.

Because she was a member of the staff, Win was given a private room and I was allowed to stay with her every day. The school holidays had just begun.

She said to me one afternoon, "Your birthday is coming soon. I haven't been able to buy you a present, but would you like my watch?"

I still have it after 36 years and it is going well.

Win deteriorated quickly, and she was eating and drinking hardly anything.

We were chatting one day about the holiday we had booked and a nurse said to me, "You do know your friend is very ill, don't you?"

I could not accept it. On Friday night, I was given an armchair to sleep in next to her bed.

At about 2 o'clock, she suddenly said, "I feel like a cup of cocoa."

The nurse immediately said, "Lovely, Win. I'll go and get you one."

Win lay back on her pillow, took a deep breath, and died. The nurse returned with the cocoa.

"I think she's gone," I mumbled and I was right.

I sat there for a short while; we had lived together for 24 years. The nurse packed Win's belongings in a black sack, and then, accompanied me to the car. As I drove home alone to the empty house, the sun was just beginning to rise.

The next few days were like a dream. Half of me had died with Win. I offered our holiday to a couple who had long been our friends, and they accepted. The following Tuesday was my birthday, I spent it with my parents.

Father was not very well and he was concerned that I had given up my holiday. I explained that I had no one to go with who could share a room and the Scilly Isles were fully booked for extra accommodation.

Win's funeral was on the following Saturday and the church was packed. Heather—the little girl we had fostered—also came. I played the piano as Win had asked.

The following day, my father contacted me. I was correct in what I had said about the Scilly Isles being fully booked, but he'd phoned one of the vicars who arranged for me to sleep in the church warden's house, but have all my meals in the hotel with my friends.

I was very surprised but agreed to join them. They agreed that I could take Sally—who meant so much to me—and she would sleep with my friends and their dog at night.

The holiday was going well, although the grief I was feeling, stayed with me, and at times, it was overwhelming. The Scilly Isles were beautiful and brought great comfort. I also had lovely memories of our previous visits and was so grateful to my father for organising it for me.

At first, the weather was good, but then it changed. The rain fell and the sea became unusually rough.

The proprietor of the hotel called me. "There has been a call from your sister, could you please ring her?"

I did immediately and was told that father was not well and he was calling for me. There was nothing I could do. Neither the ferry nor the helicopters were working because of the weather.

Two days later, she telephoned again to say that our father had died.

The end of our holiday came. I had to return home to face an empty bungalow, a life without Win, my father's death, his funeral, a grieving family and also running my school. All this had happened since the term finished in July.

Bill

My first thought when I arrived home was for my mother. She seemed to be coping well, but one of her concerns was the dog; a beautiful golden retriever also called Sally. I had always promised my father that if anything happened to him, I would take care of Sally as she was too strong for my mother.

I never imagined that Win would die at the same time and I would still be responsible for my school. The funeral for my father took place and life had to continue.

My mother felt unable to take Sally out as they lived on a main road and she could not cope with Sally on a lead. I knew I had to find a solution.

It was Sunday. Bill came for his church coffee. I had been invited out to lunch, so he was not coming home with me, but I needed to speak to him. I explained about my mother's dog and wondered if there was any way in which he could help me.

He looked thoughtful, but said nothing except, "You'll manage somehow!"

The evenings were still light and I was in the garden when Sally became excited. I went to see what she heard, and there was Bill, sitting on the dustbin holding a large black sack.

"I've come!"

He slept in my study every night, refusing the bed that was in there. All his worldly possessions were in that one sack. I fetched my mother's retriever Sally the following evening. She immediately played with my Sally, and I had never seen Bill looking so happy; his face shone!

The following morning when I got up, he had gone out with both of them. I had no idea where, but I trusted him and left for school. More than four years went by. Bill and I established a routine.

He enjoyed taking the dogs walking at night because there was hardly any traffic and would return in the morning with fresh mushrooms, blackberries and other fruits according to the season.

We called my mother's Sally *Big Sally*, and mine *Little Sally*. They would all then sleep through the day, while I was at school. If ever I took Bill out in my estate car, he always sat in the boot with the dogs.

He never got used to the phone, but if someone rang when I was out, he would pick up the receiver and say in a gruff voice, "She's not 'ere, she's out!"

I learnt that he was a prisoner in the Second World War. After he was freed, he returned to England but could not get any work. He'd walked from building site to building site, sleeping rough, and eventually, it became a habit.

In many ways, he settled in very well. Living in a building was frightening to Bill. Fortunately, my bungalow had large glass windows and patio doors. He loved the television and also read when we would sit quietly together in the lounge.

The vicar paid him for cleaning the church hall. After he had received his salary, Bill spent his money on a bottle of cider and would sit on a milk crate drinking it, in my front drive overlooking the fields on a Sunday morning. Several people asked me if I minded, which puzzled me. Why should I mind, he wasn't doing any harm?

There was one habit, however, which I never quite understood. Bill always kept his hair very short, but when there was a full moon (and it did relate to the full moon every time), he would go into the bathroom and shave his head completely bald.

I never knew what he did with the hair he cut off, there was no sign of it anywhere, and the bathroom was left spotlessly clean. Bill told me how desperately difficult it was to shave in the early days when he was on the road.

Sometimes, he asked gardeners if he could borrow their secateurs for this purpose, but they rarely let him. The only alternative was to burn his beard with matches. Then, disposable razors were introduced and Bill's life changed when he discovered them in pedal and waste bins—it was such a relief.

Bill is holding Chris my cat. On a bitterly cold winter's night just before Christmas, there was a knock at my door at 3 in the morning. It was the police telling me the burglar alarm was going off at my school in Hillshott, could I go and investigate. I went and it was a false alarm, but what was more important to me, this little black and white cat was huddled up in the light of a lamp post, trying to keep warm on that frosty, dark night. She had often wandered into the school during the day, as if lost. I could not leave her there, so brought her home in my car. We put numerous notices around the school, but no one responded, so Chris stayed with me for the rest of her life and Bill loved her.

China

It was now five months since Win had died. The New Year stretched ahead of me, there was no holiday to look forward to and nobody to plan something with. I joined a Bible study discussion group at the vicarage.

We were talking one evening and somebody mentioned holidays. A member of the group, Sally, had recently lost her husband. She realised that I would have no one to go away with.

"Why don't we go somewhere together?" she suggested.

It was a lovely idea. We studied the holiday brochures and China was mentioned. Surprisingly, it was a similar price to those nearer to home. All my connections with that country welled up.

"Sally, you wouldn't be interested in going to China would you?" She jumped at the idea. We booked up with the firm Bales for a date in June, which fitted in with my half-term. I was also graciously given an extended leave of absence by the governors.

The day before we were due to leave, we received a phone call from Bales, asking if we were still happy to go as there were developing student riots which might cause problems. They were willing to refund our money if we wanted to cancel due to the circumstances. Both Sally and I agreed to go.

We met the group at the airport, there were 19 of us and our leader Shirley. We stayed in Beijing for the first week. Apart from exploring local places of interest, we enjoyed visiting sites like the Terracotta Warriors and the Great Wall.

There were very few visitors due to the situation, and the Great Wall was almost empty which was quite unusual and very special. We had a free morning, and Sally and I decided to walk into Tiananmen Square. There was a strange atmosphere.

It was peaceful, but there were police wandering around, and at the far end a large number of students were lying down on hunger strike, beside them was an enormous placard in both Chinese and English that read:

'Mother, I am hungry, but I cannot eat.'

Near the entrance, a young artist was selling his paintings depicting various Chinese scenes and different places, they were beautiful. We told him we would come back and buy some before we left Beijing. Two days later, on Friday, we returned, and the atmosphere was totally different.

There were many more students, it was crowded and the police waved their hands at us telling us to go. We wanted to buy some illustrations from the artist. We saw him, and to our surprise, he was beckoning to us.

We went straight over and he picked up a pile of his paintings and handed them to us. We were a little confused, we could not afford all of those.

"Please, take them," he said. "Please, take them. I give them to you. There is going to be trouble and I want them to be safe."

We were bewildered as to what to do. The police came over and indicated for us to leave. We gave the artist all the loose change we had, took the paintings and left. We never saw him again, and when I look at his lovely works of art, I wonder what happened to him.

We left for Hangzhou on Sunday 4 June 1989. Early the following morning, before breakfast, Sally and I wandered down to the nearby lake to watch the Chinese practise Tai Chi. We were just starting to return to the hotel when, in the distance, we heard a strange noise.

I find it hard to describe, it was a mixture of shouting and hissing and it came nearer and nearer. Then we saw hundreds of students careering along the road, turning over barriers and tipping cars, they were all screaming, and it was deafening. We ran as fast as we could back to the hotel and Shirley, our guide, was waiting in the foyer.

"There has been a terrible, terrible massacre in Tiananmen Square. Tanks have rolled in and mown down the students, crushing them to death, and everywhere young people are protesting."

There was no mention of this whatsoever on Chinese television or radio. Shirley could not get any detailed information locally, but Kate Adie was at the square, reporting for the B.B.C. and Shirley contacted the B.B.C. World Service and the UK, by phone.

After breakfast, our group met with her in a corridor where we were hidden. We were told that—hard as it was—we could not go outside in the street. Sally and I, went up on the hotel roof and watched hundreds of students carrying banners and shouting and chanting as they protested on the roads below.

We had stayed in the hotel for three days when the proprietor told Shirley that they were beginning to run out of food, and transport for new supplies was almost impossible. We had a meeting in one of the rooms and Shirley asked us all to give her any travel vouchers we had.

She tried to get some train tickets to the nearest airport, hoping we could then fly to Hong Kong. The trains were travelling at night. We met in the reception area at 3am, the next morning.

Shirley told us we could only carry hand luggage, and it was quite difficult to decide what to take and what to leave behind. Although they were heavy and quite large, I decided to take the models I had bought of the Terracotta Warriors, even though it meant losing other belongings!

We waited quietly in the dark. Many of the group were nervous, but Sally and I seemed to take each incident as it came.

There was a grand piano in the foyer, and, for a few moments, I sat down and played it! We also both trusted Shirley. Suddenly, our Chinese guide arrived, he told us the students were setting fire to the trains, and advised us not to go. We all went back to bed.

Eventually, Shirley found a coach that would take us to the airport, we could also travel during the day and take all our luggage. We set off in the morning. There were students everywhere and they continually pulled barriers across the road to stop all vehicles.

Shirley asked a doctor and me to stand by the door of our coach. As soon as we were stopped, we opened the door. The doctor then spoke to the students telling them that he was a doctor and when he returned to England, he would tell as many people in the medical profession as he could, about the hardships of the students and the freedom they were fighting for. I then told them that I was a headteacher and would do the same in the educational field.

When they heard this they would let us through. I lost count of the number of times we were stopped, but eventually, we reached the airport. We had to wait a long time before a plane with seats to Hong Kong was available. The little airport was crowded with people trying to get away.

Suddenly, above the noise of general chatter, we heard Shirley's voice, "Bales, this way."

We jumped up as quickly as we could from where we had been sitting on a step, and started pushing our way through the crowds. It was very difficult. I had to kick a man in the stomach, as he blocked my way and would not move.

Finally, we reached the runway and raced across it as fast as we could with our luggage. We struggled up the steps and the plane took off even before the doors were closed.

When we finally arrived in Hong Kong it was deeply in mourning. Shops, buildings and all the taxis were decorated with black flags, many at half-mast.

We were met by people who gave us letters for friends in China asking if we would post them in England as they were too afraid to post them from their addresses in Hong Kong.

The people in our hotel made us very welcome, but our stay there was clouded by our recent experiences, and, in a way, we were glad to leave.

On our arrival back to England, we were surprised to be met by a crowd of people, The Bales manager and staff, our families and friends, journalists and, of course, the press.

Everyone had been so concerned for our safety, and we owed a great deal to Shirley for the way in which, with the support of our Chinese guide, she managed to find a way for us to escape.

We learnt that we were the last tourists to leave China at that time, and consequently, became the highlight of several newspapers! The headlines on the front pages ranged from:

'Our Escape from China Massacre; Head Teacher's Ordeal in China'; and 'Head Flees China Crisis.'

All were accompanied by large photos of Sally and me with detailed commentaries!

Bulgaria

The visit to China had given me much to think about and helped me to begin to enjoy life once again. I rejoined the London Emmanuel Choir.

Christmas came and I was chatting to Mrs Shepherd about the nativity play at Hillshott. The children mimed everything to music and the songs I composed. She asked me if I could bring a group to sing partway through our Westminster Hall carol services to make a break for the choir.

I thought carefully about this and discussed it with the governors. I could not possibly take the whole school but agreed to organise a group from the oldest class who were aged seven and the parents would come with us.

They sang the key songs relating to the story, dressed in the appropriate outfits: the annunciation, the journey to Bethlehem, the birth, the shepherds and the wise men.

It was a wonderful feeling for me to play the enormous concert grand piano and accompany the children who looked so tiny but sang so well to the audience of over 2,000. They received rapturous applause.

The choir—travelling as tourists—had previously visited Bulgaria when they were under Communist rule. In 1990, the system was finally abolished. It took a while for the country to adapt to its newfound freedom, especially, the Christians who had to repair—and in many cases rebuild—their churches before they could reopen them.

Mrs Shepherd—our choir leader—received an invitation for the choir to go and celebrate with them, and share in their joy at being able to worship freely again after 44 years. To my delight, I was able to go as it was arranged in August.

We stayed in a hotel and one morning to my joy, there were two golden orioles on my balcony, and they were so beautiful. I also met up and spent time with a lovely Christian family who shared with me their stories of suffering.

The father was a qualified paediatrician, but when the Communist Regime discovered he was a Christian, he was only allowed to be a dustman. He was imprisoned for his faith, and I saw the scars on his arms where he had been abused.

I went with some of the choir members to see one of the prisons where many Christians had been detained; some in a large cage. It was very dark and basic, and I found it quite frightening.

We had some wonderfully inspiring services in several of the larger churches and concert halls, and it was such a great privilege to sing with the choir. But there was one occasion I shall never forget.

I went with some of the members to a little village church. We had been invited for a reason. When we arrived, there was a crowd of people standing outside, and we joined them. A man came with a ladder and—carrying a large cross—climbed onto the roof.

He removed the hammer and sickle and reverently replaced it with the cross. I cannot put into words how moving this was, everyone clapped and praised the Lord, and many were in tears. We went inside and the service began. I was asked to take the Bible reading with an interpreter.

I went forward to the front and was just about to start when there was a rustle of paper among the congregation. They were turning over pages in exercise books where they had copied chapter after chapter from the few Bibles bought before the Communist Regime and hidden in attics or cellars.

There had been no new Bibles available for nearly 50 years. I was so touched; it was difficult to read. We left Bulgaria a few days later, with thankfulness for the freedom—we take for granted in this country—to freely share and openly appreciate our Christian faith.

Endings

One morning, for the first time in over four years, Bill did not take the dogs out because he felt unwell. When he first came to me, I tried to register him with my doctor, but they would not accept him and told me to be careful. They later apologised, apparently, they thought he was someone else.

I suggested to Bill that he see a doctor, but he strongly refused. He then staggered out of the door shouting that he was going to see the Catholic priest who was very good to him.

I waited a little while then drove to the priest's house. It was on a main road and Bill was sitting on a chair in the front garden. Later, I learnt that he refused to go indoors as the windows were small and, to him, the house was dark.

The children were passing by on their way to school and several called out, "O look, there's Bill, and Father is praying with him."

By now, Bill was well known locally. The priest saw me and said he had called an ambulance which shortly arrived. Bill refused to move. The crew explained to him that they just wanted to give him some oxygen.

"Do you know what that means?" they asked.

"'Course I do, it's what comes off the leaves," was the reply.

Finally, after much gentle persuasion, Bill agreed to go to the hospital, but you could see that he was terrified. I followed the ambulance. He was admitted straight into a ward while I waited downstairs.

They asked me for his address and who his next of kin was, and I gave them my name. A few minutes later, the sister came down to see me.

She had confirmed these details with him, and apparently, he almost exploded shouting, "She is not my next of kin, and that is not my address. I'm a man of the road."

"Is he a man of the road?" she asked "He doesn't smell."

"No," I answered with a smile. "I hope he doesn't, he has lived with me for over four years."

She looked bewildered and I explained the situation. I left Bill there, but in the morning received a call from the hospital. They asked if I could have him home as he refused to sleep in a bed and had been lying on the floor all night.

When he arrived in the ambulance, I suggested he sleep on the bed which was in the study where his belongings were, as it would be more comfortable than the floor. Surprisingly, he agreed. Bill deteriorated quickly, and late one night, he quietly died.

I was holding his hand and the dogs were both by his side. His coffin was decorated with *old man's beard* and blackberries. The church was full at his funeral, and he was buried in Datchworth churchyard. A stone was erected later inscribed with the words:

'A man of the road for 40 years.'

A donkey was sponsored in memory of him, in the Sidmouth Donkey Sanctuary. We missed him and so did the dogs.

Big and Little Sally were older now and were able to be left at home while I was at school. Eventually, Big Sally died very quickly from a stroke.

Time went on and I was beginning to think about retirement. I simply could not imagine being at home all day doing virtually nothing.

One of the parents at school—a doctor's wife—came to see me and asked if, when I retired, I would consider being a counsellor, and her husband would support me.

It came as a complete surprise, but I thought about it, discussed the idea with a counsellor—who had helped me—and decided to make enquiries.

In the meantime, I contacted the local volunteer bureau and had an interview. I was asked if I would be interested in helping someone to write his autobiography. The person concerned had recently been released from prison, and I met him on a weekly basis with a probation officer.

I recorded him as he related his life story in detail, and wrote his words down at home. Then, I shared them with him on the next visit as he was unable to read or write.

It was extremely interesting as he had a caravan on the site of Elstree Studios and met many different people including famous film stars. I missed seeing him when the *book* was complete and counted it a privilege to have taken part in its production.

Leaving the school was not easy, but I had a wonderful farewell evening organised by the governors. Teachers from the past joined us, several members came from the education authority and the inspector who had been so supportive to me. I was given a copy of a large picture of elephants painted by David Shepherd, and a small one signed by him personally which I loved. I also had a delightful pottery model of me playing the piano surrounded by a group of children. A major part of my life had finally ended.

As I left, the words of the consultant once again rang through my head, "She will never be able to work."

Little Sally finally left us through old age, and I was asked if I would give a home to a little Sheltie called Cracker, whose master had died and he had laid beside his body for four days. Of course, I did!

One of my great enjoyments was to have my two nieces Katharine and Jo—Gordon's daughters—come to stay. It was lovely to have their company and give them breakfast in bed. The one special memory we will always have is—our day visit to Iceland. We left Luton Airport at dawn and flew to Reykjavik. Having toured around this beautiful city, we were given a coach drive through the countryside and along the coast. We watched dolphins and swam in the Blue Lagoon, then finally, left for home and arrived back in Luton late on the same evening.

At a different time, their brother Tom came and stayed. He spent hours visiting the Stevenage Museum and enjoying Roman activities!

Following the idea of working as a counsellor in a G.P.'s surgery, I took a 2-year diploma, and one-year university graduation course in counselling. I was the oldest student and to my amazement was awarded a university prize! How different from my early experience 40 years previously trying to get a training for teaching. I worked for 15 years with the N.H.S. at the surgery run by the doctor who recommended me in the first place, and loved every minute. It was such a privilege to be trusted with deep personal problems and emotions, some clients had been locked in their sufferings and silence for years. Vivienne, the counsellor who had supported me in the past, became my 'supervisor', a requirement for all professional counsellors.

I heard that the local hospice was urgently needing counsellors, and agreed to help in the evenings just for a short while. I was standing by the reception desk one day, when I heard someone say a new patient had been admitted into the medical ward, she had a twin sister. Something sparked in my mind, "Her name isn't Lucy is it?" "Yes." "Does she have a twin sister called Polly?" I went straight to the nurses and asked if I could see Lucy. She was lying in bed. The only thing on the little table nearby was a photo of her and Polly dressed as angels in the Hillshott nativity play. We had a wonderful conversation and laughed as we remembered how she used to come and sit on her little chair in my room.

Lucy was waiting for a suitable heart which would enable her to have a transplant. I visited her several times and also met her mother. Sadly, the needed heart could not be found, and a few weeks later Lucy died. It was a privilege to have known her and to take part in her funeral.

Zimbabwe

My mother spent her last years in a very loving care home and I was with her when she peacefully died. She had always taken a keen interest in the work of Miriam Dean, a neighbour during her childhood.

Following the Second World War, Miriam went to the aid of refugee children abroad and her work, then progressed to Africa. My mother greatly appreciated Miriam's tireless efforts to care for children, and she spent hours sorting bags of clothes for them.

She also included tiny little clown-like dolls which she made out of black stockings; they had pointed hats to which a bell was attached. I have no idea where she got the pattern from, but I do know that—as a child—I helped her make them.

Miriam Dean's work continued as a mission, and it was no surprise to us as a family, that when my mother died she left a substantial donation to this worthy cause.

The mission asked us if we would like the money to be used for the provision of a borehole in a community in Zimbabwe which had no fresh clean water. We immediately agreed, and the work was soon underway in a tiny village called Gwava in the Masvingo region.

The following year, we received this report from those responsible for organising and drilling the borehole:

'The borehole is properly functioning and giving a high yield of water. It is the deepest of all the boreholes we have recently drilled. The people of Gwava are very committed to their work. They constructed a garden just near the borehole.'

'The garden has different varieties of vegetables and beans. Since last year, the Gwava people have generated some money to help themselves. Their garden is properly fenced such that the invading domestic animals cannot break through.'

'Life is now easier for the Gwava people since they have clean water and green vegetables every day. The presence of water has influenced these people to grow fruit trees in their gardens. The fruit trees include orange, guava and mango.'

I decided that I must go and visit Gwava to see the borehole for myself, and meet these lovely people. The Miriam Dean Mission gave me details of where to stay in Masvingo.

I also contacted Jill Dando—who had been the commentator on a recent television programme about Zimbabwe—to ask her advice about travel arrangements to this remote area. She and her secretary were very helpful and recommended a travel agent. Sadly, Jill was killed a few weeks later.

I shall never forget that first visit. Having collected together six large cases of clothes, pencils, books and toys, I arranged for Air Zimbabwe to come and collect them the week before I was leaving. This they did willingly and without any charge. I was delighted.

The day came and I set off. I left my car in a Gatwick car park free with Barclay card tokens. The flight was straight forward—13 hours through the night.

I asked for a window seat, and in the early hours of the morning, watched the sky suddenly turn from a deep black velvety hue to a glorious fiery glow. It was my first experience of an African sunrise. What a joy, what excitement, and how very beautiful.

We landed and I went through customs without any problem. Harare is a lovely, light and sunny airport, and the warm morning air filled me with happiness as I went to the exit lounge and saw a mass of smiling faces waiting to greet all the arrivals.

I waited for a moment—carefully scanning each one—searching for anything which might indicate that someone was there for me. I decided to stay in a hotel in Harare for the first day and night, before venturing forth to more remote areas.

All my arrangements had been reserved by the company that Jill Dando had recommended. There he was. A giant of a man with a shining black face and the most wonderful smile.

He was holding up a large notice *Mrs Brown*. I went straight over and he held his hand out to greet me.

"Let me take your luggage."

"Thank you, but this is only a fraction of what I have, the main part was sent on ahead by Air Zimbabwe."

"Then, we have to fetch the rest from cargo," he explained. "Follow me."

He led me outside and into another department piled high from floor to ceiling with bags and cases of all shapes and sizes.

However, will they ever find mine? I thought.

I gave my details to the officer behind the desk, and he promptly disappeared behind the mass of luggage. We waited and waited, and after what seemed like hours—in fact, it was only 10 minutes—he brought out one of my cases to be identified as mine, which I did.

"That will be (so many hundred) Zimbabwean dollars." I looked at him in disbelief.

I cannot remember the actual number of dollars, but I do know that it was the equivalent of three hundred pounds in sterling, all my spending money. I had not been given any indication that I would have to pay.

"I can't pay that amount," I meekly replied, totally dismayed.

My driver saw my utter confusion.

"They are just gifts," I explained.

"Please, open the case and see. They have been brought over by your airways free of charge."

The officer at the desk turned and spoke to my driver in Shona.

The driver translated the conversation to me, "He says you will sell them."

I vehemently protested and showed them a letter from Sister Helen at the Bondolfi Mission where I was going to stay, but it counted for nothing.

I was losing patience. I had not slept throughout the night. I was tired, hungry and felt helpless and frustrated not being able to speak the Shona language. I looked at my watch, it was 7 o'clock. The driver continued to protest on my behalf.

This continued until 1 o'clock, and by now, all my luggage was on the desk. At one point, I thought I was going to faint standing in the heat as the temperature rose. My driver had three phone calls telling him to go to other appointments where customers were waiting, but he stayed with me.

Finally, at 2:30pm, when all my cases were opened, and the contents were examined, we came to a final agreement. I would pay the equivalent of one hundred and fifty pounds in sterling.

As I imagined, and my thoughts were later confirmed, this money just went straight into the officer's pocket. I should not have paid anything.

Unfortunately, this was one negative aspect of Zimbabwe.

My driver was kindness himself, he kept apologising, although he did all he could to help me. Finally, we arrived at the Wild Geese Lodge; a hotel on the out skirts of Harare. I was quite sorry to say farewell to him, he tried so hard to stop me having to pay, and was so kind.

A porter showed me to my room, it was absolutely fascinating, with very high ceilings all made from tree trunks. I left my luggage unopened and wandered out into the beautiful grounds surrounded with showers of purple bougainvillea and radiant poinsettias eight feet high. They were so different from the tiny specimens we buy in pots at Christmas.

No sooner had I settled down on a simple wicker chair—which to my tired body, seemed like a feather bed—when a waiter approached.

He looked at least seven feet tall but had the same gentle courteous manner as my driver and a beaming smile. I soon learnt that this was indicative of the many Zimbabwean people whom I was privileged to meet.

"Can I get you a drink?"

Wonderful, I ordered a mango juice.

"May I ask, are you from the USA?"

"No, I'm from England."

"Do you know a place called Stevenage?"

I could not believe my ears. There was I, sitting in this glorious garden, watching hummingbirds in the flame trees, and a waiter was asking me if I knew Stevenage; the modern, built-up housing estate and shopping complex about three miles from where I lived!

"Yes, that is where I often do my shopping!"

His face lit up. "I wouldn't be here if it were not for Stevenage."

He must have seen the bewilderment on my face as he continued, "They paid for my education and they built our fire station."

"What here?"

"No, in Kadoma where I lived and where my family lives."

It was not until I returned home that I realised Stevenage is twinned with Kadoma, and yet I had driven passed the road sign hundreds of times! The mango juice was delicious.

Boreholes

After a delightful breakfast with the most delicious fruit, a car arrived to drive me to the Bondolfi Mission in Masvingo. There the Miriam Dean Mission had arranged for me to stay.

It was run by Catholic sisters who welcomed me so warmly I felt at home immediately. The following day, I awoke to the sound of the sisters singing in the chapel. I lay in the little bed, just listening, I felt so peaceful and happy.

Later in the morning, one of the sisters drove me in a large truck to Gwava. It was quite a distance away and very remote. I could not take my eyes off the surrounding scenery.

Parched earth stretching to the distant horizon, rutted tracks strewn with huge boulders, and women and children walking endlessly—barefoot, seemingly in the middle of nowhere—carrying pots or possessions on their heads.

As we arrived at Gwava all the villagers—many dressed in their colourful costumes—came pouring out to meet us. They were singing and dancing in a way that I had never experienced before—it was sheer joy.

I was treated with such kindness and appreciation, they found it hard to find the words to express their gratitude for the borehole and could not thank me enough. I explained it was my mother who had given it to them. The headman made a speech, and I presented him with a photograph of my parents.

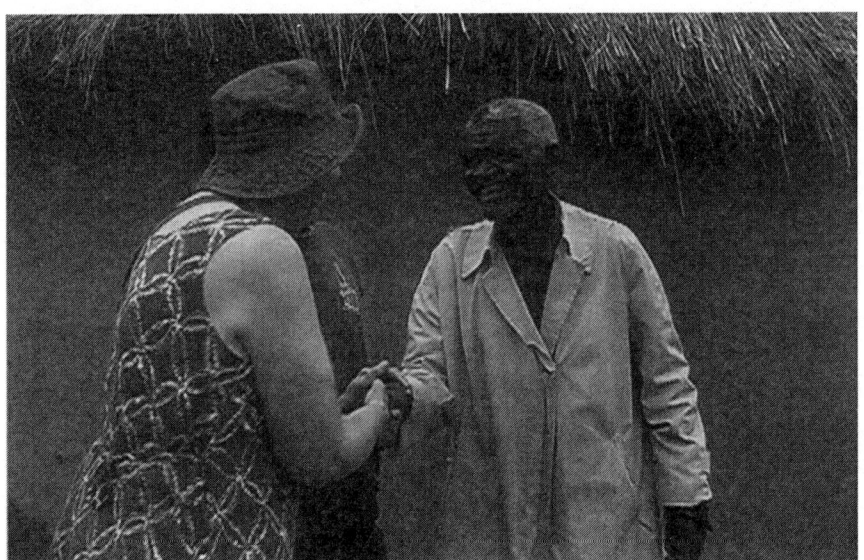

He carefully hung it on the wall in his little mud house, next to a plaque that my sister had previously sent, containing the names of our mother and father and a reference to the borehole.

The dancing, clapping and singing continued. The villagers proudly showed me the vegetables they had planted and the fruit trees they had grown. We stayed there for the whole day. It was a very special occasion which I shall never forget.

I loved my stay at Bondolfi, every day was different, and there was so much to see and learn. I visited the clinic and met people who had walked for miles and miles to come and have treatment or give birth to a baby. The electricity was very spasmodic.

One late evening, when it was dark, I went to see a mother and her newborn baby; she had just given birth. There was no electricity, so her baby was born in the light of a little gas lamp and torches, but they were both doing well.

The sisters took me out in their truck to see many villages and meet the people there. Some of them had never seen a white person before. The time finally came for me to leave. It was sad to say *goodbye*. There was a long drive to Harare Airport, but again, a car had been organised to drive me there.

Once on the plane, I sat back to relax; pondering over all I had seen. Music was being played over the Tannoy system and suddenly, the Lord's Prayer was being sung.

I looked out of the window as I listened, and it felt as if a voice was saying, "This is not your last visit, you will be coming back."

Little did I know that this was a true prophecy.

I returned to the counselling work in the surgery. The doctors and staff showed a great interest in my trip.

To my surprise, they gave me one hundred pounds, and said, "This is for your next borehole."

I was extremely grateful and my mind went back to those special thoughts on the plane. Very quickly, other people were giving me gifts of money, and it was not long before I had enough for another borehole. I prepared for my return to Zimbabwe.

It was a joy to be reunited with the sisters again. I received the same warm welcome and quickly settled down to a routine. We visited the village where the borehole was going, and I joined one of the sisters as she travelled around visiting people.

I met a little boy who had been wandering in the Bush completely lost. A sister had found him, but they could not discover where he had come from, or where he lived. He was now in the care of a family. We also visited a home where the parents had died and the children were looking after themselves.

By now, people were continually giving me money for boreholes. They also wanted to see photographs of my visits and this was not easy as I was using a rather large video camera. I then had an idea. I needed to adapt my films so others could enjoy them.

I was recommended to visit the film club at Potters Bar, and I attended one of their meetings. I was fascinated, and everyone was so helpful. I became a member and, in time, learnt to edit my films and set them to music and commentary. I bought a projector and began to show the films publicly.

There were many invitations to churches and schools. I was surprised to discover how many ladies luncheon clubs there are! The invitations came partly for interest and partly because I did not charge.

I only asked for a donation towards supplying the boreholes and people gave generously. The Rotary Club was particularly supportive, and to my complete surprise, they made me a Paul Harris Fellow at one of their meetings.

Before a borehole was drilled, the manager undertaking the work would survey the area a week before, and place a pile of stones on the exact spot where the work was to be accomplished. I felt a name was needed for our effort to raise money for this purpose and so it was called 'From Stones to Water'.

It was not long before I returned to Zimbabwe again with a case full of pencils, exercise books, children's toys, first aid equipment and food. When I arrived at the Harare Airport, the case was missing, I was so disappointed, but there was nothing I could do.

Fortunately, it was labelled with the Bondolfi address, and a week later, it was surprisingly delivered with all the contents intact.

The sisters spent a great deal of time driving me to see the boreholes, those that had already been provided and also the ones that were being installed. We went to a remote village where the work was going on. I watched with interest as they drilled down into the hard earth; it was very noisy and dusty.

All the village people crowded around with excitement and started singing and clapping with joy. We left before the work was complete in order to reach the mission in time for supper. As we sat eating, there was a knock on the door. The manager of the borehole company came in.

"I'm sorry," he said, "But the drill has hit rocks. We cannot go any deeper and there is no water. We will try again tomorrow, but it will cost more money."

I offered to pay, and he departed. Sister Helen, the mother superior, immediately said, "We must go and pray."

Everybody left the table and went to their rooms. I sat there alone, looking at the plates of half-eaten food.

After a few minutes, I decided that I too should go and pray. I went to the little chapel and quietly sat down. A large crucifix hung on the wall. I looked at it.

"Jesus when they crucified you, you cried. 'I thirst,' please, let there be water in this borehole."

I returned to the dining room and continued to eat my supper. The sisters eventually joined me.

When they had all sat down, Sister Helen said with great confidence, "Tomorrow, we shall be thanking God for the water the borehole will provide."

I wished I had her faith.

The following morning, I rose early and joined the sisters for breakfast. We were just enjoying our meal when there was a banging on the door. It was pushed open and two ladies—one with a baby—rushed in.

"Sister, Sister, there is lots and lots of water coming from the borehole."

They ran for two hours to tell us this amazing news. We all rejoiced, and Sister Helen said a thankful prayer to God. As soon as we had finished breakfast, we left in the trucks to see the borehole, taking the mothers with us. There it was—just as they had said—flowing with water.

The workmen were astonished. They were able to fix the pump and complete their job. The borehole continued to provide water constantly and never stopped.

Lilian was the head of her village. One day, she visited the Bondolfi Mission and I asked her if she had a borehole. The answer was No. They had to fetch water from a crocodile-infested river and were always fearful for the safety of the children.

I told her I might be able to get her one, but she did not answer. There was no expression of pleasure or joy, then tears ran down her face.

"Nobody will ever get us a borehole we are too far away. My grandmother said we will never have water."

She did not believe me until the day the drilling lorries moved in. Not only did the villagers benefit, but the cows also had a drinking trough. It was wonderful to see them all enjoying the cool fresh water in the heat of the day, from what came to be known as Lilian's borehole.

One morning, a sister took me to a village where a borehole was being drilled. She left me there for the day so that I would have time to meet the people and watch the work being done. Lunchtime came. An open fire was lit in the centre of the village.

Suddenly, I saw two men carrying a goat, it was dead. They threw it onto the fire and it began to cook. As I watched it sizzling away, I guessed it was for my dinner.

Charity—a teenage girl—brought a sturdy little table out from one of the mud huts, and placed it near the fire with a chair. I was then asked what part of the goat I would like to eat.

I hesitated and said, "I don't know, I have never had goat before."

They recommended the liver, which was then put on a plate and placed on the table. I sat down—somewhat apprehensively—and the villagers stood around in a large circle and watched me eat.

Then, Charity came over and spoke to me, "Only eat what you can."

I was impressed by her phraseology and command of English because the majority of the local people only spoke Shona. She had just left a basic village school. I asked her what she was going to do.

"Help my mother to look after the children," was her reply.

"What would you like to do for a career?"

"Be an accountant, but my mother could never afford the university fee for that."

Charity had no father. I could tell she was an intelligent girl, and was saddened to think it was impossible for her to have a career. Later that evening, I spoke to one of the sisters who knew her well, and she agreed with me. I finally arranged for her to go to university and study accountancy.

So, the work continued.

Uganda

In the year 2004, the foreign office advised me not to go to Zimbabwe due to the number of white farmers being shot. I had several thousand pounds from donations, saved in my African bank account. I was concerned about leaving them there when people were crying out for water.

A friend of mine—Jenny Ottewell—was working in Uganda with the Church Missionary Society. I contacted her suggesting that I went out there for a visit and financed one or two boreholes. She was delighted.

When I arrived, I was introduced to Janet; a lovely Ugandan pastoral worker who helped Jenny with the many village people they regularly visited.

On my second day, Jenny suggested that Janet would drive me to see some of the villages where there was extreme suffering and untold hardships due to a severe drought and lack of water. We set off in her truck. The ground was incredibly parched and the vegetation withering.

Men and women were desperately trying to break the brick-hard earth to find some means of planting crops, but it was impossible. We came to a small village where starving families sat listlessly on the dusty ground outside their huts; waiting and waiting for the rain to fall. There was a mother cradling her children.

She was crying out pitifully, "Our Father, who art in heaven, please, bring us food, please bring us food, hallowed be Thy name, Thy kingdom come, please, bring us food, please, bring us food. Thy will be done on earth as it is in heaven, please, bring us food, please bring us food—" her cries echoed through the hot stifling air.

Words failed me.

We could not help her, even if we had brought food with us to give away, there would never have been enough for everyone, and it would have caused riots. We drove on. A week later, I heard that she and her children had died. My heart sank and my faith wavered.

Eventually, we came to a remote, rough track. We bumped along it endlessly for what seemed like miles, and as we did so we passed children—so many children—carrying old tin cans. They were all walking in the same direction. Finally, we reached their—and our—destination, a shallow river.

Children were standing in the water filling their cans, and alongside them were cows paddling, their dung was plopping into the water the children were collecting for drinking. I spoke to them, and although they did not understand what I was saying, their smiles reflected their happiness.

Our journey continued for a very short while to the Nyakatonzi School in Kasase. The children and staff were all waiting outside to greet us, news spread fast and we were expected! The noise of cheering and singing was deafening.

Janet and I finally wended our way into the school, and I was introduced to the headteacher, the governors and the headman. They all had prepared speeches. The headteacher explained how the children got headaches, sickness and diarrhoea from drinking dirty water, and some developed cholera and died.

At this point, a young boy—aged about 10—stood up and told us how he and his friend had got cholera from drinking this dirty water; he lived, but his friend had died. Janet then told everyone present that a borehole was going to be installed in the playground providing fresh water for them all.

There was immediate singing and dancing which just went on and on! Finally, and somewhat reluctantly, we left. A few weeks later, I received a photograph of the completed borehole with a group of children drinking the clean water.

Gifts for my forthcoming 70th birthday provided a small motorcycle for Anna—the headteacher—so that, she could safely travel the three miles to school while carrying books and money which could not be left there (previously she had to walk).

It also enabled her to quickly ride around and check the cows and their owners who were linked with the 'Send a Cow' charity.

The money I had brought with me, also provided a borehole for a refugee camp in Lango, Lira, Northern Uganda. Children were being kept there in safety, away from soldiers who were abducting them for the army. I was not able to visit the camp, but Janet went on the day the borehole was finally completed.

She sent me an e-mail:

'I bring greetings from all of us at Lango…the children treasure your generous contribution…Okello, one of the teachers remarked, "It is true, God gives life."'

On several occasions, Jenny took me to the nearby market. It was buzzing with activity and full of colour, although fruit and vegetables were scarce due to the drought. I noticed smoke rising in one corner and went to investigate.

A witch doctor was brewing his medical concoctions. I moved closer to see what he was actually doing. Jenny came rushing over, physically grabbed me and pulled me away.

"Never, never go near a witch doctor, you can never underestimate his power and the damage he can do."

I learnt my lesson!

Jenny regularly travelled to the villages to take services, and she invited me to join her. I remember one in particular. It was held in a large mud hut with a straw roof, and only women attended. I sat near the one who was sobbing, and, through her tears, she explained that two of her sisters had died.

She was unable to go to the first sister's funeral as she was nursing the second sister at the same time until she too died. Many of the women spoke English as a second language, and they asked me if I would teach them a hymn we sang in England.

I thought quickly for a moment, and the verses of 'Brother, sister let me serve you—' came into my mind. Fortunately, I managed to remember the words, and they loved learning them and singing them along with me:

"We are pilgrims on a journey and companions on the road, we are here to help each other walk the mile and bear the load. I will weep when you are weeping when you laugh I'll laugh with you, I will share your joy and sorrow 'til we've seen this journey through."

Whenever I hear that hymn, my thoughts immediately return to that moving little service, with those dear women in that mud hut. If ever I am asked to choose a hymn, I nearly always choose that one.

My time in Uganda came to an end. It was comparatively short—and the only visit I made—but it left a lasting impression on my mind which I will never forget. The following year, I was able to return to Zimbabwe.

Filming Abroad

I was amazed at the number of different groups who invited me to show my films on Zimbabwe, and then, invited me back for return visits.

I realised I would have to extend my repertoire as I depended on these meetings for financing the boreholes. I contacted the travel firm recommended by Jill Dando and they were extremely helpful. I would focus on wildlife.

My first expedition was to Borneo. I had a wonderful time filming the orangutans with their young ones; such beautiful, intelligent animals. Then, there were proboscis monkeys in the jungles; their calls were echoing through the trees. I had my own individual guide who was extremely helpful.

He sat patiently waiting with me hour by hour until I had the shots I wanted. There were only two occasions when he became frustrated. Because of my back, I was unable to climb a rope ladder to see the bats clinging to the roof of a cave.

On another occasion, we sailed in a little boat to a tiny island where baby turtles were just hatching from their eggs on the white sandy beaches; some were racing into the sea with their parents.

We arrived in the boat, and the owner dragged it to the shore, and then, told me to jump down onto the sand. I could not, my back had no flexibility and my body would have jarred. The guide complained that he had not been told that I was disabled, but of course, he had not had this information because I had not given it!

At home, it was important to focus on the things I could do, and work around or avoid the things I found difficult. I just forgot about any limitations, and would never have thought of mentioning them in my application.

It is so different when you are in completely strange surroundings; the one problem when on holiday! Finally, two men lifted me over the edge of the boat and dropped me onto the sand. It was painful, but at least, I got there!

The turtles were a joy, watching them scuttling down to the sea in the moonlight was such a beautiful experience and, something, I shall never forget.

India was another excursion. I found this difficult. The Taj Mahal was magnificent, but the poverty upset me. Children without hands begged for money. Next door to our luxurious hotel was a huge rubbish dump where young and old were scrabbling for food.

As we sailed down the Ganges, cremation fires on the bank burnt dead bodies, their flames and smoke rose, polluting the air. This time, I was travelling with a group. Several of us fell ill.

I was taken to a clinic in a tuk-tuk and carried over a cow lying on the floor in the doorway, cows were sacred. The nurse, dressed in the most beautiful sari, gave me a long drink of water-like liquid. I have no idea what it was.

"You will be better in three hours," she assured me.

I was well enough to return to the hotel and eat the evening meal! Rats were discovered in the kitchen, there was also a rat trap in my bedroom! The condition of the dogs worried me. So many wandered in the streets looking for food, some with tiny puppies trying to suck drips of milk from their half-starved mothers.

I was thankful when we moved on to Nepal. This was—to me—a gentler country with beautiful butterflies and flowers. I visited a school with a hundred children in one class all sitting on benches. They stood up as we walked in and greeted us with such respect.

Another interesting place was the birthplace of Buddha. So many sights and sounds to film.

Patagonia was also recommended by the travel agency; an incredible visit. The wild scenery as we approached the Andes mountains was awe-inspiring, and glaciers towered above us as we sailed our way through icebergs.

The wind—which howled around in some of the flatter areas—was quite frightening. We were shown how to lie down, if necessary, to save us from being literally blown off our feet. Then, there were the penguins. How I just loved filming the Magellanic penguins; hundreds of them.

We stayed on their site for nearly a week; closely observing them on icy ground. I was able to film inside a penguin's mouth as she stood sleeping. She was upright and motionless, but opening and closing her beak as if snoring.

Those days were special: silently watching the penguins so closely, being among them, seeing their nests, watching their movements, listening to their calls and being almost overcome with the magnificent sight of them waddling into the sea in their hundreds. A wonderful trip, and one which enabled me to obtain the IAC LACI award for my films.

I was able to make a number of films on elephants. On visiting a friend in Thailand, I spent a complete day riding on the back of an elephant. I was entirely alone apart from the guide.

We trundled through forests, paddled along streams and ploughed our way across a river with water rising above the elephant's thighs and reaching my feet. While I was in Thailand, I also decided to treat myself to a luxurious weekend by staying in the Oriental Hotel, which was renowned for being one of the best hotels in the world. Indeed, it was quite beautiful in every way.

On another trip, I spent several days in an elephant camp in Zimbabwe. On this occasion a friend came with me and we helped wash and feed the elephants. I was able to film inside an elephant's mouth when he was being offered a sweetmeat by the keeper.

At other times, I filmed elephants alongside a variety of different safari animals. On one particular occasion, there were a number of babies with their mothers. It was a privilege to watch and record.

Some of these films were shown in St Neots Cineworld during a film festival.

On one of my visits to Zimbabwe, I visited the Victoria Falls and was even able to walk a little way across the mighty outpouring of water.

These trips, and other, more ordinary ones, enabled me to build up my film selection, and raise the extra money needed for boreholes.

A Slight Setback

One of the disadvantages of visiting the villages in Zimbabwe was the lack of toilets; we just had to squat on the ground. I began to notice that when I got up, one of my hips seemed slightly locked. On my return home, I was referred to a consultant.

Although a minor operation would have temporarily resolved the problem, he recommended a complete hip replacement, and I agreed.

Following the surgery in a private hospital, I was told the operation had been very successful, and the next day, a nurse helped me out of bed and asked me to stand. It proved impossible, my leg felt completely weak and limp; it gave away, and I fell over.

I tried again, but the same thing happened, I lay back on the bed. The consultant came to see me, he was mystified. I was given physiotherapy and hydrotherapy, but they made little difference. Reluctantly, I was finally sent home walking very slowly and totally relying on two crutches.

Friends whose hips were previously far worse than mine, were able to play tennis and walk freely without any discomfort after their hip replacements. They came to see me. I knew something had gone seriously wrong.

I bought a powered chair which gave me some freedom and enabled me to take my little dog Cracker for walks. He was very good and faithfully followed me along the lanes.

The weeks passed and there was no improvement. The consultant operated again, but it did not help. I was transferred to the Stanmore branch of the Royal Orthopaedic Hospital and received pioneering surgery which involved transferring a nerve, but this too failed.

Finally, I was given a second complete hip replacement and then sent to the Great Portland St branch for intense physiotherapy. As I approached the main entrance, memories came flooding back.

I paused for a moment, and the friend helping me, held my arm and asked, "Are you all right?"

"Just thinking and remembering."

The last time I walked up those steps was over 50 years ago. We made our way to the physiotherapy department. At least this time, they would not be hanging me by my neck to try and straighten my spine!

My childhood polio was now considered as one of the possibilities causing the failure of my recent surgery. I continued attending Great Portland Street for many months, it was like old times!

One day, for some reason, I wandered to another part of the hospital and found a long corridor where photos of past consultants were displayed.

I stopped, and thought, *could he be there*?

I searched along the many portraits, and, yes, there he was. There was no mistake. I stood looking at his face, and his eyes stared back at me.

I could hear his voice, "She will always be a problem for the dressmaker and she will never be able to work."

A shiver went down my spine. I lingered for a moment, then, quickly moved on.

The hospital finally discharged me with little improvement. I had become accustomed to walking with crutches, and fortunately, could drive my car, which was adapted with a hoist so my powered chair could be transported if necessary.

My thoughts now turned to Zimbabwe. Having made a few enquiries about travelling as a disabled person, I set off on my next journey. I booked an assistant when I bought my ticket, and sure enough, a porter was there at Gatwick Airport with a wheelchair when I arrived.

After going through the customs, he took me to a luxurious waiting room for disabled people. At the appropriate time, I was pushed to the plane, bypassed the queue and went on first, and an air hostess helped me up the steps.

On arrival at the Harare Airport, I was met by another porter who wheeled me to collect my luggage. He took me through customs, and finally, pushed me to the meeting point. A driver was waiting there to take me to Bondolfi.

The sisters gave me an especially warm welcome and looked after me with such care that there was absolutely nothing to worry about.

When we travelled in their truck to visit various boreholes, they supported me as I climbed up onto the high front seat which proved an advantage for my comfort. The villagers greeted me with exceptional warmth, and I almost forgot that there might be difficulties.

The whole visit was full of joy. It was a wonderful time and gave me the confidence to return to Bondolfi again on many occasions.

On one visit, there was a slight incident on my way out, which caused brief concern. I carried the money for the boreholes with me rather than trying to transfer it through the bank, which could create problems in Zimbabwe.

On this particular occasion, my hand luggage went through the scan and I was called over. The porter pushed me to a side room where I was questioned about the £5000 in my bag. Fortunately, I was prepared.

I had my recent bank statements with me, an electricity bill with my name and address and, of course, my passport. After explaining what the money was for, they were perfectly willing for me to take it and board the plane.

The porter who was pushing me waited patiently outside, he was very concerned and asked me if I had been carrying drugs. I assured him that was not the case and all was well. He looked positively relieved!

There was just one occasion on a visit to Zimbabwe following the surgery when I became particularly anxious. We were driving out in the bush, heading for a remote village. There were no roads and we had to go through a very rough area.

Suddenly, the truck got stuck in some long grass and shrubbery. The village we were visiting was still a long way off, and realising I could not walk, I wondered what was going to happen to me. I did not want to be left in the truck all night!

The sisters set off walking, and I waited alone for hours. Darkness fell, and there was no twilight in Zimbabwe, then, at last, I heard the sound of voices.

The sisters returned with a group of men who—with an almighty push—freed the truck and we were able to drive home. We successfully visited the village again the following day, without any difficulty.

So, in spite of my crutches, and with the support and help from many friends, the work with the boreholes in Zimbabwe still continued; supplying fresh water to villages, schools and churches.

The Nursing Care Home

Although I had adapted to my slightly different way of life, there was one experience which vividly remained with me for a long time.

When I was due to leave the hospital following the second hip surgery, there was concern about my returning to an empty house and living on my own. It was decided to send me to a nursing home for a few days, but all the local ones were full, and it seemed there was not a spare bed anywhere.

Finally, a room was found and an ambulance came to take me. On arrival, the driver wheeled me into the reception area where a number of patients were sitting.

I smiled and said, "Hello."

But no one answered. I was greeted with complete silence, taken upstairs in a lift, and shown into a tiny room. The door on the wardrobe was hanging on its hinges. There was no remote control for the little old television, so you could not change the channels.

The bed was small and hard; only two foot six in width. A member of staff told me to undress even though it was only 3 o'clock in the afternoon. She took away all my clothes and belongings including my handbag with money, but, surprisingly, let me keep my mobile phone.

Before I put my nightdress on, she wrote my initials DB in large capital letters on the back of the neck. I sat on the bed, the chair beside it was too low for my newly acquired hip. It was not long before another member of staff came and told me that I was going to have a shower.

I was then wheeled to the lift on a commode and taken into a toilet area on the lower floor. A kettle was boiling on a shelf. My night dress was pulled off, and I was told to get up, which I did with difficulty.

Then, I had to stand naked, facing a tiled wall, pressing the palms of both my hands on the shiny surface. The member of staff poured steaming hot water from the kettle into a bowl and tipped it over me.

I cried out as it burnt my shoulders and back. She roughly dried me with a towel, pulled my night dress back on, and took me back to my room. I sat there just waiting and wondering what would happen next.

Then, tea was brought in with a watery, half-poached egg, on a soggy piece of toast. I tried to watch the television but was unable to change the channel or alter the volume, and could only switch it on and off.

At half past 6, I was told to get into bed. It was so narrow; they put bars up on both sides, drew the curtains, turned out the light and left the door open. The cries began.

On and on people were calling out, crying, "Help, help."

Finally, after an hour, someone came to my room.

"Please, could I have the door closed?" I asked.

"No," was the quick response, "We're not allowed to close the doors."

About 2 o'clock, she returned and switched my light on.

"Oh please," I cried. "It is so bright, must you put it on?"

"Yes, I've got to check that you are not dead."

Morning finally came. I felt stiff and just hoped the bed had not damaged my hip. I decided to get up and have a wash, but there was no plug in the basin, the hot tap was not working and the cold was only a trickle. I could not stay here; who could help me?

I rang my brother David who was my next of kin, but he was not available. Then, I remembered one of the members of the film club—I belonged to—lived reasonably nearby. I had his number and phoned him.

Within a short while, he arrived in his large car with a friend, and somehow, found his way to my room. He half carried me out to a back door, still wearing my nightdress, but the manager saw him and told him to stop.

He continued and his friend waylaid the manager asking for all my belongings. Suddenly, a nurse appeared and she knew me; a lovely girl from Zimbabwe whom I had met at church.

"Auntie Daphne, whatever are you doing here, this isn't the place for you?"

The manager looked totally bewildered and let me go. I returned home safely—still in my nightdress—and all my belongings were intact.

A few days later, I made further enquiries about the home. It was for people suffering from severe dementia. On reporting my experience to social services, both the manager and his deputy were replaced and the home was completely transformed.

My Zimbabwean friend—who incidentally was only there on that morning as a supply—told me it was a totally different place now. I think I was meant to go there!

Following the final surgery, my niece Emma stayed with me and gave me all the care I needed.

Harare

Apart from staying in the Bondolfi Mission, sometimes, I spent a few days with John and Ketani Matiza and their children who live in Harare. I had met them a number of years previously when they came to England for John to take a theological course, and we attended the same church.

John appreciated that my main concern for the provision of water was focused on the remote villages in Masvingo. He also explained to me the desperate need in some of the Harare schools. On one of my stopovers, I suggested that he took me to see the situation for myself.

Within a few minutes, I was in his car and he was taking me to the Kubatana School. There were two thousand pupils and no water for toilets, washing or drinking. On the way, we drove past Mugabe's palatial home. Soldiers stood on guard outside with rifles poised ready to shoot at any moment if needed.

"Quick," said John. "Hide your camera and don't look at them."

For a moment, I felt quite frightened. On arrival at the school, John showed me where they had tried to dig a well by hand, but the ground was rocky and it was impossible. On my return home, I mentioned this school to a friend, and he paid for a borehole to be provided in memory of his mother who had recently died. It was called the 'Ruby borehole' after her.

Drilling boreholes in the Masvingo area became increasingly difficult due to the lack of diesel, but the money was still coming in and everyone was happy for me to use it to provide water wherever it was needed. On my next visit, I spent longer with the Matizas.

I returned to the Kubatana School and saw the Ruby borehole which was working well; supplying clean fresh water for all the pupils and staff. I also spent time chatting with over one hundred orphaned children as they queued up for their one meal of the day.

I had taken money for a borehole in another Harare school. Similar to Kubatana, it had over two thousand pupils, and there was no water. I went into the toilets, and the smell was overwhelming. Opposite the school, there was a large field of cabbages.

John told me that there was a pool at the far end, but it was filled with dirty water. I decided to go and see it, just out of interest. As I walked, I noticed that my sandals were making a squelching sound and my crutches were slipping.

I looked down, and to my horror saw the ground between the cabbages was thick with human excrement. Whether it was there for fertilisation, or whether it was where the children went if they could not face the toilets, I do not know, but I turned back and left the pool! The borehole was drilled in the school a few months later.

On further visits, water was provided in Molife Primary School and Mukombi and St Judes secondary schools; each with well over one thousand pupils who—prior to the borehole installation—were suffering from cholera. I was also privileged to spend a day at Fungai Vamwe Preschool Centre for orphaned children.

There again a borehole had been drilled. I watched fascinated as these little ones lined up in an orderly fashion; patiently waiting for their turn to collect a drink of water in their cupped hands. John also told me about the desperate need for fresh water in the poorer parts of Harare.

In some places, people were pulling up the manhole covers in the streets and collecting water from the drains and even the sewers. We discussed the situation, but there was a problem. If a borehole was drilled in a public place, no one would be in charge.

I always stipulated that there must be someone who was responsible for the upkeep of each borehole. It was usually the headman in a village. In the case of a school, it would be the headmaster.

Then, we had an idea. Three boreholes were provided and they were drilled alongside churches. The pastor, or members of the congregation were responsible for their upkeep, and access for the general public was easy.

In 2008, there was a terrible shortage of food due to the devaluation of the Zimbabwean dollar. Many friends from Datchworth and elsewhere were very generous and enabled me to send out food to the Matiza family; both for themselves and also for the orphaned children in the schools.

Five Zimbabwean men—three based in England and two in Zimbabwe—voluntarily organised the transport of this food. They provided second-hand barrels which had previously been used for mango chutney in Zimbabwe, and delivered four to my garage.

Different people helped to fill them with a variety of food including powdered and baby milk, tea, soup, pasta, flour, cereals and many more items. They were then collected by the men and shipped to Zimbabwe. The two men in Harare received them and took them to the Matizas. So, we knew everything had finally arrived safely.

When I returned for my next visit, food was slightly more available, but even so, Ketani had to queue for three hours for a loaf of bread which she purchased for my benefit. The rural areas were suffering terribly.

As I was driven from Harare to Masvingo—a journey of nearly two hundred miles—I noticed that all along the route, women were digging around tree trunks.

I asked the driver what they were doing, and he told me they were looking for tree roots to eat as there was no other food.

There was a tremendous contrast in the homes of people living in Harare, and I had the privilege of visiting both the rich and poor. I spent one day with a wealthy Zimbabwean family who owned a large cotton factory from the time the country was known as Rhodesia.

They had a beautiful house and garden, surrounded by high railings for safety. We were relaxing by their swimming pool and enjoying the afternoon sun, when suddenly, there was a shout by the railings and a large sack was thrown over, it landed on a flower bed.

My hostess remained unperturbed and explained to me what had happened. The sack was full of peanuts, it belonged to a street vendor. Street vendors were forbidden in Harare, but some people were so poor, they risked being caught.

When the police were seen coming, my friend gave the vendors permission to throw their wares into her garden and she would mind them until it was safe for them to be collected later.

One afternoon, two brothers came to visit me at the Matiza's house and asked if I could pay for medical treatment which their sister Mary desperately needed. She was suffering from a large facial tumour which distorted her whole face. Her mouth and teeth were almost touching her eyes.

The tumour could not be treated in Zimbabwe and their only hope was to send her to South Africa. I was very strict about all the money that was given for the provision of water and ensured that every penny was used for that purpose.

The disappointment on their faces—when I told them I was unable to help—left me with both sadness and guilt. I watched them walk away despondently knowing all their hope in me was lost, and there was nothing else they could do.

When I eventually returned home, I could not get the expression on the faces of those brothers out of my mind, and the thought of their sister who was unable to get any medical help or treatment. She had just left school and wanted to be a doctor.

I suddenly remembered how one of the members of the Datchworth village church had said to me, "If ever you need any money for something else other than water let me know."

I told him about Mary, and the following day, a cheque for one thousand pounds was put through my letter box. Mary's brothers had told me that the cost of treatment in South Africa would be exactly that amount.

The money was safely transferred via John Matiza, and Mary was able to go to South Africa. Sadly, the treatment failed and she returned home with little improvement.

One night, I lay in bed, thinking and thinking about her, and praying that somehow, I might find a way to help this young girl. Quietly, but clearly, a memory emerged of a documentary film I had seen, 'The Boy David'.

It was about a little boy in Peru who had been found wandering in the jungle with a terrible facial deformity. He was brought over to England, given surgery and adopted by the consultant. A charity was then set up to help children with similar conditions.

I got out of bed, looked on the internet and found that Professor Iain Hutchison performed surgery free of charge for such cases at St Bartholomew's Hospital. He also founded the charity 'Saving Faces'.

The next morning, I contacted his secretary, and a few days later, he telephoned me personally. Lengthy and detailed communication took place between doctors in South Africa, Harare and St Bartholomew's Hospital involving letters, photographs and detailed medical records.

Mary's family raised the money for her stay in the hospital, and Air Zimbabwe agreed to fly both her and her mother over to England without charging them. Professor Hutchison performed the major surgery.

It was a huge tumour, her whole face, mouth, nose and eyes were affected, but he carried out the operation successfully and cared for her throughout the whole procedure and recovery without any cost. I visited her several times and, finally, she returned home as a different person—well and so happy.

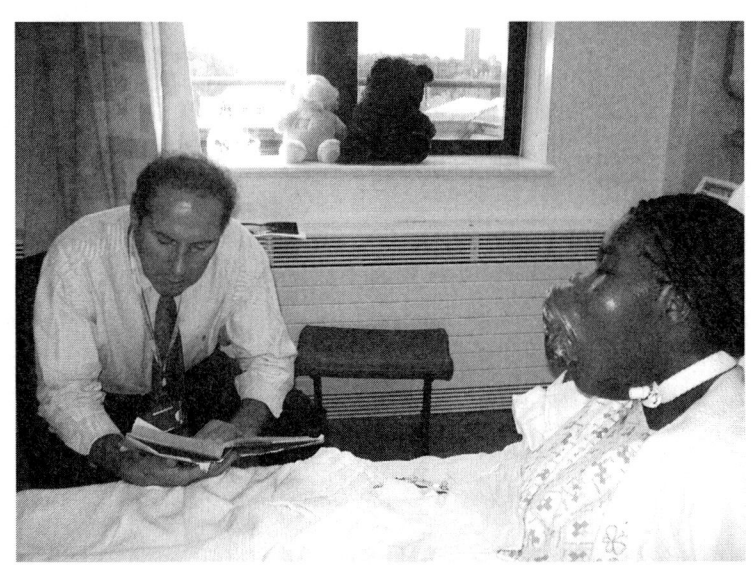

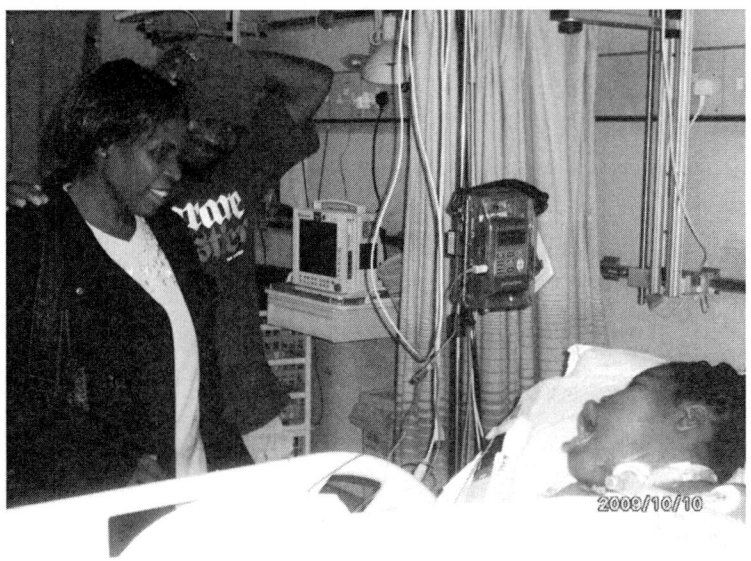

A New Beginning

When my fourth hip surgery failed and my walking became weaker, I realised the time had come when I could no longer care for my large garden and it was time to move to somewhere smaller.

The thought of leaving Datchworth—having lived there for 46 years—filled me with apprehension, but I decided it would be sensible to be near my brother and sister-in-law David and Joyce who lived in St Neots, and my nieces Marina and Emma, who lived nearby.

I so loved my bungalow with its garden and large patio doors overlooking the open countryside, and the glorious radiant sunsets. I felt I would never find anywhere that could compare with its beauty.

One night when I lay awake thinking, and wondering what I should do, I decided to look on the internet and see if there was any apartment for sale in the St Neots area, overlooking water. I had often stayed with David and Joyce and had always appreciated the peace and tranquillity of the River Ouse.

Sitting there in my nightdress, I fiddled around with the computer keys, and there it was; a ground floor apartment overlooking a marina in Eynesbury which adjoined St Neots. The following day, I drove to see it.

Although I had no appointment, the lady owner invited me in, I could hardly believe what I was seeing. Large patio doors in almost every room, with the most wonderful views of the marina which joined the River Ouse and came right up to my patio wall.

Beyond the water, there was an extensive green conservation area with trees, backed by a wide expanse of sky and, yes, the patio doors faced west—sunsets!

Two swans gracefully glided along, I could almost touch them, and a cormorant violently shook its feathered wings as it perched on one of the moorings.

Within a few minutes, I turned to the owner and said, "I'll have it, but I would like my family to see it first."

They came the next day, and Marina said, "Your bungalow in Datchworth looks out on a beautiful picture, this looks out onto a beautiful film."

My decision was final. I contacted the housing agent near Datchworth, and within three days, my bungalow had been sold.

Goodbye was hard: I would miss the many friends I had made over the years and my links with the church. Also, the school where I had been a governor and helped with the music, but one of the greatest losses was my work as a counsellor. I had been attached to the surgery in Letchworth for 15 years.

It was such a privilege to work with those who were broken with grief, lost and confused, lonely, frightened, sad, abused and abusers, homosexuals and transgenders. Listening to their life stories without judgement, and above all, gaining their trust. Everyone was different, and I learnt so much.

It was the August bank holiday weekend. A removal lorry arrived and most of my belongings were packed inside. It then waited and parked outside the bungalow throughout the night.

Early the following morning, I slowly walked round my beloved garden for the last time, then, wandered into each room as the removal team transferred my remaining possessions into their vehicle. I closed the front door and turned the key *goodbye*.

The journey to St Neots took about 45 minutes. I drove in my car alone, ahead of the removal van and reached the apartment without any problem. The next few days were spent unpacking boxes, and trying to organise spaces for all their contents.

I was so grateful to my family and many friends who came to help. On Sunday, I went to the nearest church, which belonged to the Methodist denomination. It reminded me of my childhood days during the evacuation; bringing back fond memories of aunties who took me to a similar place of worship.

I told the visiting minister I had just moved into the area and she said, "You, come here, they'll take care of you."

That has proved to be so true.

I soon felt at home in the church. I joined almost every group so that I could get to know people, but one of the greatest joys was when—after only two weeks—the organist discovered I could play the piano and invited me to accompany him with the hymns during the services.

We quickly developed a rapport and enjoyed music together, not only playing hymns but also giving concerts which included pieces from the musicals and a variety of other classical and light compositions. Our theme tune was the Dam Busters March!

One thing I missed was my visits to the Gordon Craig theatre in Stevenage, near to where I used to live. I had been a *friend* of the theatre for many years, and on occasions, the children from my school had performed on the stage. But now, it was some distance away.

The local U3A organised theatre trips, so when they held an open day, I went to make enquiries and hopefully join. I knew they arranged trips to London theatres and looked forward to taking part.

Enthusiastically, I found the appropriate table and spoke to the person in charge, then, without any hesitation, asked if I could join.

To my utter amazement, she looked at my crutches and said, "I'm sorry but we couldn't take you."

It had never occurred to me that I might be turned down. She explained to me that, sometimes, they are unable to park near a theatre and walking is involved.

Also, some of the theatres are quite old, and a number of stairs have to be climbed in order to reach the seats. I understood what she was saying, and left—sad and disappointed.

Having come from a village where I knew almost everyone, it was quite difficult adjusting to a place where everybody was a stranger. However, there were some surprising little links with my past.

My niece Marina, lived in Blunham, a few miles away from Eynesbury, and her children attended the local school. Three weeks after I had moved in, they invited me to the harvest festival which was held in their village church.

At the end of the service, the vicar—a mature-looking lady—spoke to everyone as they left and, realising that she had not met me before, asked if I was visiting. I explained I had just moved to the area and she enquired as to where I had come from. We then had the following conversation:

"I've come from Hertfordshire."

"Whereabouts in Hertfordshire."

"Oh, a tiny village called Datchworth, you've probably never heard of it."

"Oh yes, I did know someone who lived there, her name was Daphne Brown, did you ever meet her?"

I gave a wry smile, "Yes, I did actually."

"If you see her do give her my regards," I just laughed.

"You can give her your regards yourself, she is me!"

She gasped, "You were my headmistress!"

I could hardly believe it, we both looked at each other, we seemed about the same age! I was immediately introduced to the members of the congregation who were still there, and consequently, on all the future occasions when I attended the church.

"This is Miss Brown, she was my headmistress at Hillshott school. I was in her nativity play!"

That must have been over 40 years ago.

Not long after, a couple moved into one of the apartments above me. Their daughter came to visit and she met me in the entrance hall.

She looked at me and said, "I know you, you're Miss Brown."

I paused, wondering and she continued, "You used to teach me music at school."

"What, at Hillshott?" I queried.

"No, Datchworth."

For several years, I had taught music when I was a governor in the village school, and she remembered and recognised me—amazing. On another occasion, a new resident arrived.

In conversation, she mentioned she had lived in Letchworth when she was a child. I asked her where she went to school—*Hillshott*! It was a long time after I had retired, but there, once again, was the link.

Walking in my powered chair with my little Sheltie dog Honey, was a joy. We only had to cut through a car park and we were in a grassy conservation area alongside the marina.

We regularly passed a house where a large cat sat by the front door watching the world go by. One day, the door suddenly opened and some children came out. I asked them what the cat's name was.

"Daphne!" they said.

I immediately told them that was my name.

From then onwards, whenever they saw me, they would wave and call out, "Hello, Daphne."

Frequently, they came over to my chair and talked to me, including the teenage boy who I thought was so kind. One afternoon, their mother was with them and I said how much I had appreciated her children's friendliness.

She told me they had only moved there recently and it was nice to have someone to talk to. I asked where they had come from, and the answer was *Letchworth*!

"Where did the children go to school?"

"Hillshott. Why? Do you know it?"

No wonder, they were so friendly! We had a wonderful evening; sharing photographs and experiences, mine from long ago, theirs during the previous year. Sadly, they moved away shortly afterwards.

For many years, I had arranged for help with the cleaning in my bungalow, and I knew, I must find someone to assist me in a similar way with my apartment. I did not know of anyone who could help me and had no contacts to follow up.

A card however had been put in my post box advertising a cleaning company, so, I decided to phone them. They told me there was a new person who was available and they would arrange for her to visit me. The day came, and at the appointed time, she arrived.

As she walked up the steps to my front door I went out to meet her and smiled.

"Are you from Zimbabwe?" I asked.

Her eyes widened, and she asked, "How did you know?"

We had so much to share and talk about. Her name was Rue and she started working for me immediately. In time, her husband Tendai came and helped me with planting on my patio and any manual tasks that needed doing. As time went on, Rue left the company and was employed by me privately.

When they first came, there were three children in the family, Shantel, Justin and Shanon, but later, twins arrived—Jaylen and Jayden. Sadly, there were difficulties with their birth, and Jayden developed both physical and mental problems.

By now, we were all as one family. Tendai and Rue called me Mum, and the children called me Granny. Jayden was nearly three years old, but he was still not walking or talking. One day, Tendai and Rue brought him over to see me on his own.

Suddenly, he got up and began stumbling out of the patio door to look at the ducks, he then started to say a few words, we could hardly believe it, and we felt like crying. Jayden often came to see me until he started at a special school; he both walked and talked on every visit.

Another little boy then arrived, Jamal. Sometimes, he accompanied Tendai and Rue when they came each Friday. It was such a delight for me to have grandchildren and their parents did everything they could to help me.

Back to Zimbabwe

Charles—one of the members of the Methodist church—came from Zimbabwe. So, I very quickly got to know him. He told me of the lack of fresh water in Marondera where he came from and where his family lived.

Every year, our church raised money for a particular need, and when they heard Charles and me discussing his situation, they unanimously agreed to provide £4,000—the cost of a borehole to be drilled near his family home.

Within a few months, the amount had increased to £12,000 and, although I had been out to Harare only a few months earlier, I, very willingly agreed to make the necessary arrangements and travel to Marondera with the money. Charles arranged for me to stay with his mother and brother.

Shortly before I was due to leave, I received an e-mail from Charity, inviting me to her graduation. The ceremony would be held at the African University in Mutare, where she had finally completed her chartered accountant training.

I was thrilled to receive the invitation, but could not imagine how I would ever travel to Mutare. I spoke to Charles and could hardly believe his response. His brother's wife was a lecturer at the university and she would arrange for me to travel from Marondera and stay with her overnight. How amazing!

I arrived safely with the £12,000 in my purse attached to my waist. Charles' brother met me at the airport and his mother—a lovely little lady—made me so welcome in her bungalow. The following day, they took me to the two schools where boreholes were going to be drilled.

As we drove along, I saw women and children—miles from anywhere—walking through scrubland with large containers on their heads as they went to collect water. On Sunday, we went to Dombotombo church; the local Methodist church where Charles' family worshipped.

The third borehole was going to be placed on the church grounds where the general public in Marondera would have access to clean fresh water. I found the service very moving. The church was a large substantial building and it was packed to its full capacity.

There was a choir dressed in bright red outfits, and some of the members accompanied the hymns playing on kudu antelope horns.

When it came to the time for the offertory, the plates were placed on the communion table and everyone in the congregation stood up and queued in a long line all around the church. Slowly, they walked forward, placed their money on the plates as they passed by, and then returned to their seats.

Sometimes, they remained silent, but then, would suddenly burst into singing and dancing. I was fascinated. After the service—which was about two hours long—a group of women cooked a chicken for me on an open fire. I was so touched. Then, they took the saucepans away to wash them in a river. A few weeks later, after I returned home.

I received this email:

'20 August 2011 12:38 p.m. They completed drilling the Dombotombo Methodist church borehole three hours ago. It was such a great joy to watch the underground water gush out with such tremendous force.'

'I tell you, the sight of the hard-to-obtain, life-sustaining liquid brought smiles to the faces of the crowd that stood to watch.'

The day came for Charity's graduation. Charles' brother drove me to Mutare. It was a journey of nearly one hundred miles, and his sister-in-law met me. I shall never forget that day.

The ceremony was held in the open, but an imposing canopy sheltered a large platform on which the presentations took place. The university caters for over one thousand students and they were all present alongside the same number of guests packed together on the tiered seating which surrounded the area.

I was graciously given a reserved place on a chair in the front row—and, to my delight—Charity's mother was sitting next to me. It was an interesting experience being the only white face amongst so many.

A programme was given to me with the names of the *distinguished guests of honour*, they included: government ministers, ambassadors, bishops, mayors, members of the senate and many others.

The procedure started, the chancellor and chairman of the Africa University Board of Directors and several other dignitaries came onto the platform dressed in rich crimson robes and elaborate headboards, and then, the speeches began. Eventually, the time came for the presentations.

I could see Charity lining up and, finally, her turn arrived. I was almost in tears as I watched this young girl receiving her graduation certificate in the presence of so many people on such an auspicious occasion.

My mind went back to Spambe her little village, where they cooked a goat for me, and her words, "Only eat what you can."

I felt so proud of her. Afterwards, we met up. What a joyous occasion. Charity introduced me to some of her friends who were so lovely. Then, I left to stay the night in a university apartment which had been reserved by Charles' sister-in-law, and returned to Marondera the following day.

The time came for me to return home. I felt sad leaving Charles' family, especially, his mother; they had been so kind. It was early evening when I boarded the plane at Harare Airport, and we set off on—what was now for me—a very familiar journey.

Suddenly, there was an announcement from the pilot, "Unfortunately, we have to make an emergency landing in Lagos Nigeria. Due to volcanic ash, we are no longer allowed to fly any further."

The plane landed. Doors opened, and the air hostesses ushered everyone out, but of course, I could only walk a little way with my crutches. They came to help me and I was taken off the plane by another exit somewhere near the luggage department, so, I did not have to cope with so many steps.

One of the hostesses fetched a wheelchair and pushed me to a reception area where the other passengers were waiting. We were all given a piece of paper on which was written the name of a hotel. Everyone seemed to be comparing notes.

There were several in the group who knew the hotels and were making comments about them.

One of them looked at mine and said, "Oh that is not good, try and get it changed."

My heart sank. Suddenly, we were all told to go to a different reception area. Everyone moved and I was left behind in the wheelchair. Some of the passengers offered to push me, but then declined, because of insurance; afraid there might be an accident. I was left in silence.

It seemed as if everyone had disappeared. I was not afraid but felt concerned that I may have been forgotten and wondered how long I would have to stay there alone. After an hour, a porter appeared and told me he was taking me to where the others were waiting outside for minibuses to transport them to the hotels.

It was good to see the group again, and several seemed quite pleased to see me! The minibuses came, and everyone crowded on, but I could not manage the high steps. A driver tried to lift me up, but it was useless, and finally, they drove off without me.

I shall never forget the feeling; I had been left there all on my own. It was a huge parking area, a massive stretch of tarmac, entirely empty, and completely void of cars, not a person in sight anywhere. I looked at my watch, it was just 3 o'clock in the morning.

I gazed at the vast expanse of black sky with myriad twinkling stars; silence, complete silence. Where was everyone? All I could do was sit and wait. I could not move the wheelchair. I could not walk any distance. I was helpless.

Suddenly, I heard the sound of a car approaching and headlights pierced the darkness as it hurtled into sight and drew up beside me. The driver got out and helped me move from the wheelchair. I had no idea where he had come from or who he was.

I struggled into the front seat and, within minutes, we were careering through the streets of Lagos as if being chased. I had no idea where we were going. The piece of paper with a hotel name on it was lost, and we seemed to go on and on.

I did not know where he was from, or who he was, I just hoped and prayed he was taking me to somewhere safe. At last, we slowed down and stopped in front of a large hotel on a busy main street. He helped me out and assisted me to the main doors, where a receptionist welcomed me in.

All I had was a little hand luggage, the rest of my belongings had been left at the airport. I just stood for a moment taking in the scene before me. The hotel was palatial. After showing my passport and registering, I was taken in the lift to my room.

It was luxurious: the bed was laden with the softest of pillows, the whole decor was rich in colour with golden trimmings, and the shower was lined with marble. The receptionist told me that I would be woken at eight. I only had four hours to sleep, no time for a shower, and no time to wallow in the comfort of the hotel.

I am not sure if it was the one originally written on my slip of paper, but as I had lost this piece of information I would never know. Promptly, at 8 o'clock, the phone by my bed rang and the operator informed me it was time to rise.

I was so sleepy, but managed to dress and go down to the restaurant for breakfast. The first thing I noticed was the tables. They all had glass tops under which freshly picked rose petals were laid with such care, and scattered to form a velvet-like covering.

I then turned to the breakfast buffet which stretched for the whole length of the large airy room. I have stayed in hotels of high quality before but never experienced the assortment and array of fresh fruit displayed there before my eyes; it was difficult to know where to begin.

At 10 o'clock, the minibuses returned to take everyone back to the airport, but, once again, I was unable to climb into the vehicle.

Fortunately, this time, the hotel ordered a car almost immediately and I arrived at the same time as the others. The journey continued without any further problems. We safely reached Gatwick and all our luggage was intact.

In spite of the difficulties experienced in this last particular journey, I continued to return to Zimbabwe on a number of occasions; visiting friends in Harare and the Bondolfi Mission. However, the cost of providing a borehole was rapidly increasing.

When I started this work, I paid £1,500 for each one, but by 2016, the drilling companies were charging £7000, mainly due to the cost of diesel. I began to wonder how much longer I could continue. Many people had supported the work financially for a long time, was it fair to keep on expecting more money?

Then, the answer came in a very unexpected way. Polio had affected my lungs. Although breathing had always been a slight problem, it never really interfered with my way of life. However, I was beginning to have difficulties at night and the hospital consultant issued me with a Nippy ventilator.

This meant I had to wear a mask when I slept, with a tube attached to the machine that blew air into my lungs making breathing much easier. It proved to be a considerable help, but had to be plugged into a mains socket, and relied on an electricity supply.

In Zimbabwe, the electricity frequently shuts off at night. It might also be quite difficult to transport the Nippy machine—which is cumbersome and would cause complications when carrying it through customs—especially if I was relying on a porter to help me.

Sadly, I realised my days to visit Zimbabwe were over. I felt sad to think that I may never see the sisters again. The Matizas might possibly come to England.

However, it was the warmth and friendship of the people I continually met, and came to love, that I treasured so greatly. I can never thank them enough for the joy they have given to me.

Because of the generosity and support of so many, in 17 years, it has been possible to drill 42 boreholes as follows.

1999 Gwava Village, Masvingo (Cost £1,500 each) Mihwa Village.
2000 Chirove village, Masvingo Nzembe village, Masvingo.
2003 Mutoredzanawa village, Masvingo Masvingise village, Masvingo.
2004 Nyakatonzi School, Kasese (Uganda) Lango Lira refugee camp (Uganda).
2006 Bondolfi Mission, Masvingo Spambe village, Masvingo Lilian's village, Masvingo.
2008 Kubatana school, Harare Molife school, Harare Mukombi school, Harare St Judes school, Juru, and
Ruwa church, for the community, Harare Budiriro church, for the community, Harare.
2010 Three housing estates in Harare.
2011 Dombotombo Methodist church, for the community, Marondera Nyameni Primary School, Marondera.
Nyameni Secondary School, Marondera Chivi village, Masvingo.
2012 Rusike village, Juru Chitungwiza village, Juru.
2013 Zengaza village, Juru Mukombami village, Juru Gosha primary school, Harare, and
Kandava Secondary School, Harare.
2014 Mwacheta village, Chipinge, Juru Musirizwi Ruwadzano,
Sakuinje village, Harare suburb, and
Hatfield Church, Harare, for the Community Chipangura School, Harare.
2015 four villages in Masvingo (they now have numbers instead of names) 2016 three villages in Masvingo (cost £7000 each).

Hostel for Young People

I was quickly making new friends and enjoyed exploring the beautiful local scenery, but I missed my counselling work.

A few weeks after my arrival, I was in church one Sunday morning and was introduced to someone who worked at a local hostel for homeless young people. I asked if the residents had any contact with a counsellor.

I was told that this was a huge problem, as their only link was through the Mental Health Association and there was often a two- or tree-month waiting list. I casually mentioned my interest in counselling and wondered if I could be of any help.

Within a week, I was interviewed and then, attended a short course which dealt with incidents such as bomb threats, drug dealing, abuse and theft. Three weeks later, I saw my first client.

I was allocated a tiny room adjoining the secretary's office. It was simply furnished with two chairs and a small table. The staff told the residents when I was available, and then, they decided whether they wanted to see me or not. I soon had a waiting list.

The work was different from the surgery. All the residents were aged between 16 and 25. They were each provided with a bedroom, and for communal use, there were showers, a billiard and recreation room, a kitchen for providing their own meals and a computer room where a member of staff taught reading and mathematics.

My first appointment was at 11, sometimes, the client would sleepily arrive in his or her pyjamas, but most of them came dressed and reasonably on time. Many of them had lived rough, some had been in prison.

One client—a very pleasant 19-year-old—proudly told me he had qualifications in plumbing, cooking and carpentry. He asked me if I would like to see his certificates. I said I would love to, and he could hardly leave me quickly enough to fetch them.

Dashing up the stairs to his room, he returned within minutes holding the treasured pieces of paper in his hand. In my innocence, I asked him if he had earned them at school or college.

"Oh no," was the reply. "In prison. I want to go back if I can and am trying to work out what I can do to get convicted, I could try breaking into a shop."

A number of the residents had been in care, one client had 14 foster parents, and nearly all had lost hope, lacked confidence and found it hard to trust people. The Prince's Trust was brilliant. It gave them a purpose in life and enabled them to leave with a qualification and a future career.

In spite of the common factor of homelessness, every case I worked with, was very different. Once again, I counted it a privilege to be trusted with the deep, complicated experiences of these young people. Listening to their side of their life story was spellbinding.

I was saddened by the number of disillusioned adults who said to me, "How can you spend so long with these young people who are just wasting time and causing trouble?"

Sometimes, I did wonder how I could possibly help them. Many had been turned out of school before their time, and very few had any qualifications. In the world, as it is today, it was hard for them to make any progress. But there was always hope, sometimes, it failed, and sometimes, it succeeded.

Pete (I have changed his name) came into the room for his first session with me. He was about six feet tall and in his late teens. He slumped into the chair, put his feet on the table and ignored me completely.

I asked him to confirm his name.

"Pete."

"And when is your birthday, Pete? How old are you?"

"2 August."

"Oh Pete," I responded in an excited tone. "Say that again."

His whole attitude changed, his feet came off the table, he half stood up and he yelled back at me, "No one ever listens to what I say, no one ever understands me."

He raised his arms in the air and shook his fists at me.

"Pete, Pete, I only asked you to say it again because it's my birthday too and I wanted to make sure I had heard you correctly."

His whole attitude instantly changed.

"Cool, well done, Mate."

He slapped my hand, then sat down and relaxed. From then on, Pete and I related really well. He felt totally unwanted by the outside world including his family, except for his grandmother who—he believed—loved him.

He was convinced that when you die, your body disintegrates, but your brain lives on, and that is what he wanted to happen to him.

We spent hours discussing suicide and he assured me that he always felt better when he left our sessions and wanted to carry on living. One day, however, I arrived at the hostel and a group of residents were waiting for me at the main door.

"Pete tried to kill himself on Friday, but it didn't work. He's been in hospital all weekend, he's back now and wants to see you."

I saw Pete and hoped he felt a little more positive at the end of the session, at least, he left with a smile. That afternoon, a social worker came from the hospital and spent time with him. She had to use my room, so, I waited in the adjoining office and could hear almost every word that was being said.

Pete was shouting at her as he did to me on that very first session. Finally, the door opened, the social worker left and Pete went up to his room. I saw two more clients, then, when the room was empty there was a knock at the door.

Pete burst in, and flung his arms around me. "Thank you, thank you, please, carry on with what you are doing."

He left before I could say anything, making for the main front door. I called out for someone to follow him, but by the time anyone had heard, he was gone. Pete threw himself over the large bridge in the busy main street of St Neots.

No one tried to stop him, but some said they heard him crying out, "Help," as he drowned in the fast-flowing river.

His body was found several days later and, during that lapse of time, several of the residents spent hours looking for him. The crematorium was packed at his service and I had an opportunity to speak to his grandmother who—he often said—was the only one who cared about him. I sent her a card on 2 August.

Sarah (not her real name) remained in school until the sixth form, she had successfully passed a number of exams. Sarah loved flowers and longed to be a florist, but her parents wanted her to go to university.

Begrudgingly she complied with their wishes and tried to study *advertising*, but it became too much for her and she had a complete breakdown. She left university, and—not wanting to return home—applied for a room at the hostel.

After I had seen her for a few weeks, and heard about her longing to work with flowers, I made a suggestion. A delightful Dutch lady in my church was responsible for all the flower arrangements and prepared them on a Thursday morning. I asked Sarah if she would like to meet Jannie.

I explained that she would have to go to the church quite independently, because, as her counsellor, I could not be part of the visits. Sarah sounded enthusiastic. The Thursday morning came, and Jannie was looking forward to meeting her.

It was pouring with rain, but even so, Sarah found her way to the church and arrived on time. Not only did she help with the church flowers, but also came away with her own little arrangement for the hostel, which everyone appreciated.

Sarah continued doing this for several months, and then sadly, Jannie's husband suddenly died in the local bank when he was paying in the church money. It was a terrible shock to the community, he was well-loved by many.

Jannie asked Sarah if she would be responsible for all the flower arrangements in the church for the funeral—which was such a compliment—and Sarah was so pleased to accept. Eventually, she left the hostel and successfully set up her own florist business. The last I heard, it was doing well.

Dogs

Dogs have always meant a great deal to me in my life. Little Sally was my one constant companion throughout Win's illness and death, and when I left Hillshott. But she was beginning to show her age and I wondered how long I would have her.

This little dog had meant so much to me at such difficult times, and I never ceased to be thankful that she was not returned to the dogs' home when we first had her. I had to have surgery for cancer and was in bed recovering when Sally became ill.

She was lying on her bed near mine and seemingly unable to walk, I could not let her suffer. I phoned the vet who came with a nurse prepared to put her out of her misery.

The vet knelt down beside Sally, with the syringe in her hand, and stroking her gently said, "I don't like doing this when your mum is so poorly."

At this, Sally struggled to her feet and walked out through an open door into the garden! She lived for another three years and we both recovered well!

Eventually, Little Sally died naturally from old age. At the time my mother was in a care home, and when I told them what had happened, one of the staff immediately asked me if I could give a home to a little Sheltie.

His name was Cracker, and he had been found lying in a field beside the dead body of his master. The weather was freezing cold and the ground was icy, but he had been lying there for four days.

How could I say no? I went and fetched him from the foster home where he was staying. He was a very affectionate little dog and loved my nieces when they came to stay, and they loved him too.

I still have a letter from Katharine which she wrote 25 years ago saying:

'Please, give my love to Cracker.'

It was during this time that I had a problem with my hip and had to start using a powered chair. Cracker adapted to it without any problem when going out on walks. A friend of mine, Margaret, had three shelties and belonged to the Sheltie Club.

When I went abroad she would mind Cracker. Eventually, the time came for this dear little dog to leave us, she was quietly put to sleep.

A few days later, I had a recorded message on my answer phone, "Hello, Daphne, my name is Honey. I'm a little Sheltie looking for a home, I'm six years old, could you help me?"

It was Margaret. She had made enquiries at the Sheltie Club and located Honey!

I went and saw Honey, she was in a breeding cage, a beautiful little dog with smiling eyes just like Cracker. I fell in love with her immediately. She belonged to someone who both bred and showed shelties, and Honey's mother had won several Crufts awards.

Honey herself had entered Crufts but not won anything and she was now considered too old for breeding. I took her home. We had a lovely life together. Honey took to my powered chair immediately, and, apart from daily walks, we enjoyed many holidays together.

She was a very good traveller. Eventually, we both moved to the apartment in St Neots. She adapted to having a comparatively small patio in place of a large garden and would lie for hours looking through the railings watching the ducks and swans on the marina below.

Honey was 13 and slowing down, but still happy and contented. We were sitting on the patio in the sun. It was a warm day, but the doors were all open and she could have walked into the cool shade at any time.

I got up to go indoors and called her to come with me. She was lying by my chair and did not move. I thought she was still asleep. I called again, then looked closer; she had quietly died. A lovely peaceful end for a special little dog, but for me it was so sad.

I missed Honey, enormously. The apartment was silent and empty. A few days went by, and I started to flick through the internet to see what older dogs needed homes. I did not want a puppy because of my age. My mind went back to my first little dog Scamp.

I had always been attracted to Yorkshire Terriers, they were such characters. Day after day, I looked to see if there were any available, and then I saw two, a brother and sister in a dog's home on the other side of London.

They appeared so forlorn in the photograph, and, although I knew I could not have two, I decided to phone those who were caring for them. Although they were related, they had been separated as the brother bullied the sister.

Their previous owner was an alcoholic and spent the majority of his time in bed, and the neighbours fed his dogs. A forever home had been found for the boy, but they were still looking for one for the girl, named Molly.

She was eight years old and, at present, in a foster home. I said I was interested in having her, so, a recognised local dog trainer came to my apartment to meet me and inspect the suitability of the premises.

She was lovely, very encouraging and positive and so pleased to find someone who wanted an old dog. A friend took me to see Molly the following week. She was in a private home with six other dogs, and as soon as we entered the room, she jumped up on top of the back of a sofa with fear.

I loved her, this poor frightened little Yorkie. They had asked me to bring a lead and collar, so I took Honey's collar with the address and phone number attached. The foster mother lifted Molly down, and she put the collar and lead on her.

But Molly was shaking and refused to leave the room. We carried her out to the car and I sat nursing her while my friend drove. Molly trembled with fear the whole way home. As soon as we arrived, I opened the doors and let her out on the patio.

To my horror, she went straight to the railings and squeezed through the bars. I never imagined this would happen, they were only four inches apart. Away she ran as fast as her little legs could carry her and disappeared into the distant maze of paths and roads between the blocks of apartments.

I stood for a moment, transfixed, shocked, and speechless. Then, I started to shout, but no one heard me. I could not run or try to chase her, what could I do? I was so thankful that, at least, she had a collar on with my address and telephone number.

I went to my neighbours and they willingly came out and set off to look for her. I phoned the lady who had previously checked my apartment, and she drove over in her car to join the search.

It was October, the afternoon was drawing to a close, slowly darkness fell and everybody finally returned to their homes having reassured me that someone would find Molly eventually and take her in. I sat, wondering and thinking. I could not eat.

She was in a completely strange area, lost and totally alone and such a nervous, frightened little dog. The clock ticked on. I kept going out on the patio and looking and looking at the orange glow between the dark shadows of the street lamps, but there was nothing, not a single movement. It was 9 o'clock, suddenly, the telephone rang.

I picked up the receiver, and a lady's voice spoke, "Have you lost a little dog?"

"Yes," I could hardly get the words out.

"We have her here. I am the manager of Poppyfields, the local residential care home. I have just returned to my office after doing the rounds and found this little dog sitting on a chair by my desk."

"How she got in, I have no idea as the front door is locked and you can only open it with a code. We have had no visitors this evening, it is an entire mystery, but she looks quite happy!"

With intense relief, I explained the situation and went and collected her immediately. It was true, she looked perfectly happy sitting on a cushioned chair in the manager's office. To this day, we have absolutely no idea how she got in, but I was so thankful that she was safe and had the collar on.

We returned home together and Molly spent the night on my sofa. A neighbour fastened wired netting across all the railings the following morning, and everyone who had searched the night before was delighted and intrigued by the news.

After her somewhat dramatic start, Molly settled in well. She loved sitting beside me on the sofa, and in the apartment, she was relaxed and happy. She never left my side. When we went out, she would walk as close as she could to my powered chair, and there was no need to put her on a lead.

Molly would never venture over to meet other dogs or people. If they came to greet her, she would politely ignore them. I took her on several holidays, but the one which will always remain a vivid memory was when we spent a week in Norfolk.

Molly seemed so well, and on one particular day, we walked for two hours along the headland, but she was beginning to develop a cough. The time came for us to return home, little did I know that would be my very last holiday. Molly's cough worsened.

Anti-biotics helped, but there was fluid in her lungs, and one Sunday she just could not stop choking. Our local vet was closed, so, I telephoned the animal hospital a few miles away. The person I spoke to was very helpful and told me to bring her over that evening when a vet would see her.

As so often on these occasions Molly's cough promptly improved, I took her out for a walk and she was fine. I almost decided not to go but went just to have her checked. We arrived and sat in the waiting room.

The vet called us in. He asked me what the problem was, but sounded very abrupt and did not want to hear any details. Picking Molly up he carried her into a back room, as they left she looked at me with terrified brown eyes and began shaking. They eventually returned, he stood her on the table, and she hurled herself into my arms, petrified.

"You will have to leave her here tonight and we'll give her some oxygen."

"I can't leave her. Can I stay?"

"No," was the firm answer.

I tried to explain the situation but he would not listen, he just interrupted me, "You either leave her or have her put down."

I could not believe what I was hearing.

"I'll just take her."

"No, you leave her here for treatment or I will put her down."

Looking back at the situation, I think I should have left her, but the thought was such a shock I could not face it.

I quietly said, "You will have to put her down then, I cannot leave her she will be so scared."

I do not think he expected my decision, in fact, I believe he only made the alternative suggestion in order to persuade me to leave her, but he wasted no time. Syringe in hand and he inserted the needle.

"She is gone. Do you want her cremated?"

I mumbled, "Yes."

I gave her one long last look and left alone clasping her collar and lead. As I paid one hundred pounds at the desk, a nurse came out. I had no idea that there was a nurse. If I had known, I may have had the courage to leave Molly. I went out to the empty car.

It was pouring with rain, I silently drove home in a dream and faced the empty apartment in tears. The following day, the local veterinary surgeon rang me. The hospital had informed them as to what had happened, and when I told them the details they asked to see me.

A case was brought up concerning the whole experience and I received an apology. The only positive aspect was that Molly had fluid in her lungs and it was increasing.

She would probably have lived for only another few months and was saved from suffering and severe loss of breath which would eventually have caused her death.

The easiest way of describing how I found my next little dog is to record some conversations I had when I phoned a Yorkshire Terrier rescue centre a week after Molly had died.

"Is that the Yorkshire Terrier rescue centre?"

"Yes."

"Do you have any little dogs needing a home?"

"There is one coming in on Monday?"

"How old is he?"

"Why?"

"Because I'm in my 80s and I'm looking for an older dog."

"80 isn't old, I've given lots of dogs to people of your age, they make the best owners. The dog coming in is eight. Phone me on Monday."

"Do you want my details?"

"No, you're going to phone me, I'm not going to phone you."

The phone was put down. Monday came. I waited until the afternoon, then phoned again.

"Yes, I've got him here. His name is Chocolate. His master has died and the mistress doesn't like him. He's been in kennels for a month."

"You can come and get him, but you can't come tomorrow as I'm going to see my daughter. You can't come on Wednesday as I've got a hospital appointment. You can come on Thursday afternoon."

I asked for her address which she gave to me and then she put the phone down. I was totally confused. She had not asked me for any details, there was no mention of my home being checked, it was quite confusing. A friend offered to come with me and we set off on a Thursday afternoon.

Eventually, we found the address, it was just a private semi-detached house in a cul-de-sac; nothing like a dog rescue centre. The front garden was completely overgrown, and there were blinds drawn across all the windows.

We rang the front doorbell and waited, but nobody came. We rang it again, had we got the correct address? Then suddenly, we heard a shuffling sound coming from within. The door opened very slowly, and an extremely elderly lady peeped out.

"We've come to see the little dog called Chocolate," I explained.

To this, she replied, "I was hoping you wouldn't come."

My heart sank, had we made a wasted journey?

She continued, "I can't find my glasses, so, I can't do any of the paperwork. Anyway, as you're here you'd better come in."

I cannot describe in words what we saw. Her slippers were covered in dog poo, there were piles of dog baskets stacked up littering the hall, and when she opened the first door on the left—which we discovered was a sitting room—a massive swarm of flies flew out to greet us.

We worked our way through various pieces of antique sofas and armchairs, and there—sitting all alone on an old grey sofa—sat the dearest little Yorkshire Terrier looking quite bewildered.

We were invited to sit somewhere, so while my friend found an armchair with an empty space, I settled myself down beside this delightful tiny dog.

The hostess told me she had been involved in judging Yorkshire Terriers, and she thought Chocolate was a well-bred little dog. He had a difficult time since his master died. So, she would be pleased for us to take him.

However, because she could not find her glasses, she could not do any of the necessary paperwork, but when she found them, she promised to send them on to us. I asked her if we should pay anything, and was told the usual donation towards the Yorkshire Terrier Rescue was 50 pounds.

I handed her the amount, my friend picked up Chocolate—as I was unable to because of my crutches—and we went to the car leaving behind us a multitude of flies. Chocky sat on her lap as good as gold, but my friend found it quite difficult as he was filthy.

His fur was tangled with a dried grey liquid, and as soon as we got home, we bathed him in the kitchen sink. He took it all in his stride. Right from the beginning, Chocolate—who soon became known as Chocky—was very friendly and he quickly settled in well. I was so pleased to have him.

The days went by, but there was no information from the lady who gave him to us. I decided to contact the Kennel Club and they, in turn—because of my report—decided to go and inspect her house, but there was no reply. Finally, they discovered she was in hospital.

A week later, her daughter sent me Chocolate's birth certificate and a vet's medical report. She also enclosed a letter of apology for the delay and explained that her mother had died.

The medical report had the details of the vet who had cared for Chocolate since his birth. So, I phoned them and asked them to let his previous owners know that he now had a good and happy home.

The person I spoke to paused and then said, "I know this is not very professional to say, but Chocolate belonged to the husband and the wife hated him. She couldn't get rid of him quickly enough when his master died, there would be no point in telling her."

"It was always sad as he is a dear little dog, and we were very fond of him at the surgery."

I echo her words, "Chocky was a joy. He loved everyone and everyone loved him, he just loved life."

March 2020. The Sunday morning service had taken place as normal and I had enjoyed playing for the hymns. The minister said a closing prayer and people looked as if they were ready to leave when she asked everyone to remain seated.

Then, she quietly told us that due to the recent new deadly virus, older members were advised not to attend church during the next few weeks until it had subsided. I was stunned.

I had heard about this virus on the television but did not think it would affect me, and I certainly had never ever known a minister, vicar or priest telling members of their congregation not to come to church. It was bewildering.

Afterwards, over coffee, she emphasised how serious it was, and that we must stay away from any gathering of people. The following day, I received a telephone call from the hostel with the same message. I could not go there until the virus was totally under control.

I hoped it would be for just a few weeks, but little did I know that the restriction would continue for nearly two years and, in fact sadly, I would never return to the hostel again.

Lockdown 2020

As I watched the television day after day, it became more and more obvious that the strange new virus—which had come to Britain from China—was very dangerous and spreading quickly. Everyone over 70 years of age was advised to completely isolate and stay indoors.

At first, I thought this was acceptable as I had plenty of things to do at home. I had my little Yorkshire Terrier Chocky for company and had just received my usual food delivery from Tescos. I imagined the restriction was only for a week or two.

Tendai could no longer come and help me. Rue had flown to Zimbabwe to visit a sister, and was unable to return to England; leaving Tendai to care for their six children.

Suddenly, an unexpected phone call came from Papworth Hospital asking me if my breathing was comfortable, and was the Nippy breathing ventilator—I used at night—working satisfactorily.

I said, "Yes."

I was given an emergency number to use if I needed help. They emphasised that on no account must I go out of doors or have any physical contact with anyone. A parcel was delivered the following day marked urgent and confidential.

It was a heart communicator which would monitor my heart and let Papworth know if all was well without my having to go in as a patient. I was given instructions over the phone as to how to assemble it.

We were advised on the television not to touch anything that had been touched by anyone else from outside such as the post, parcel deliveries or door handles. Those should be left for a week, then wiped with disinfectant.

Someone on the television said it was thought that everyone in their 80s or 90s would catch the virus and probably die. It was frightening.

Two weeks went by, and I was running out of food. I tried to order some online from Tescos as I normally did, but there were no spaces anywhere.

I was told that many of the shelves in Tescos were empty as people were panic buying, but my family, church friends and neighbours offered to get me anything I urgently needed if it was available.

They would then leave the items on my doorstep and when they had gone I would pick them up wearing disposable rubber gloves, wipe them with disinfected wipes, and then, wash my hands. I was getting desperate for proper food.

The following week, my doorbell rang. I looked out of my window and a man was walking towards the gate with a white box.

I opened my patio door and he called out, "Are you Daphne? I've got a present for you, where shall I put it?"

"Leave it on the seat on my patio," I shouted and watched at a distance from my patio door. "What is it?"

"My wife has set up a group to make cakes for anyone who is living alone and who has been nominated."

"Who nominated me?"

"I can't tell you, it's anonymous," he said and left.

Wearing gloves, I picked up the box and took it inside, there were words written on the lid:

'With love from Angel Pie. We hope these will cheer you up at this difficult time.'

Inside, there were eight delicious homemade cakes. I was so touched by this unexpected kindness, that I cried. I had to find out who nominated me.

After various enquiries, I discovered it was someone in the church, she belonged to a local theatre group that was organising the cooking. I couldn't thank them enough.

A week later, there was a knock on my front door. I called out, but there was no answer. Cautiously, I put my gloves and mask on and tentatively opened the door. There, in the entrance hall, was a huge box addressed to me. In no way could I lift it.

So, slowly, little by little, I pushed it inside. Still wearing my gloves, I opened it and inside there was enough food to feed two people for two months!

A huge white cut loaf, porridge, cornflakes, tins of soup, long-life milk, potatoes, carrots, an onion as big as a football, oranges, apples, coffee, tea, toilet rolls, hand wash, a massive bag of pasta and tins of meat. Enclosed was a letter from the government addressing me as a vulnerable person.

I was quite overcome with the whole arrangement and, to this day, I have no idea who actually packed and supplied the food. When I had finally unloaded it, it filled the whole of my kitchen worktop.

The enclosed letter said that if you did not want to receive another food parcel, go online and complete a form. For this, they gave the details. I did this immediately, saying how grateful I was for the generous box of food, but I did not require any more. The following Friday, to my surprise, there was a similar knock at my door, but again no one called out.

Cautiously, I opened it. I could not believe my eyes, there was another box full of identical food! I left it outside with a large note asking people in the apartment block to help themselves!

A very helpful lady in Huntingdon District Council telephoned me asking if I needed anything. She gave me a number to ring for priority slots with Tescos who agreed to deliver food leaving it on the doorstep as long as my door was closed and I made no contact with them.

This worked well. I then unpacked everything with gloves on and wiped the contents with disinfectant.

I received many phone calls during this time, and friends came to my gate. I was able to briefly shout to them from my patio door and we could just about hear what each other was saying. That was the only physical human contact I had.

Having lived alone for over 30 years I had learnt to fill the gap of companionship and love by reaching out to others. But now, I was prevented from doing this and my life was empty; nothing, nobody there. I could not venture out to meet anyone, and it was going on for weeks and weeks, months and months—it was frightening.

I woke up every morning and my immediate thought was there was nothing to get up for except my little dog Chocky. Day after day, nearly everything on the television was focused on the virus, on suffering and death for thousands. When would it be my turn?

I began to dream and have nightmares and often woke each morning shaking as I used to in the war during air raids. No one was there to help me. No one to touch me or give me a hug, just speak to me face to face. I had to cope totally alone. I decided I must do something to help myself.

A leaflet had been delivered through my door from the Rotary Club with a phone number to ring if anyone needed shopping, prescriptions or a friendly phone call, I turned it over and there they were asking for volunteers. With my counselling experience, I could volunteer for *friendly phone calls*.

I rang the number, and the person I spoke to sounded interested and, said, they would contact me in the next few days. I shall never forget that afternoon, because I felt so happy at the prospect of supporting people once again. I sat down and played the piano for the first time since this situation had begun.

I banged away at Beethoven, melted into Grieg and Chopin, and then, drifted into 'Somewhere Over the Rainbow'. The last piece had a special significance. The rainbow had become the symbol of hope at this time. Children would colour rainbows and paste them on windows.

A little card was put in my post box with the words:

"We cannot appreciate the rainbow until we have gone through the rain."

I stuck it on my front door. I continued playing and playing, then suddenly, stopped. Silence, no one was listening, no one was commenting, just silence—no one was there. I packed my music up. The Rotary telephoned me the following day to say that they had so many volunteers they could not take on any more; they did not need me.

A text came from a neighbour sending me a *virtual hug*. I queried the word *virtual* and looked it up in the dictionary and online:

'In essence or effect, although not formally or actually.'

It seemed, from that day onwards, everything was *virtual*. Zoom meetings became a major part of our contact with other people. My church organised Zoom services every Sunday, which was a great help. It was a joy to see and talk to my friends, once again, but it was not the same as being with them.

Singing hymns alone in my study was monotonous, even though I had the accompaniment of those singing on the screen. I missed playing the piano too. After an hour, the service was switched off and, just like the television, everyone had gone, and the interminable silence returned.

A few months passed when there was a nationwide agreement to go outside your house on Thursday evenings at 8 o'clock in the evening and clap for a few minutes in appreciation for all those working in the N.H.S.

Those five minutes on my patio were the only time I physically heard my neighbours for weeks and weeks, but I could not see them.

On 8 May we celebrated the 75th anniversary of V. E. Day. On the television there were many programmes relating to the war, the bombing, the blitz and the evacuees. I watched as children carrying gas masks waved goodbye to their parents and my own memories came flooding back.

Somehow, it all linked with what was happening now, separated from family and friends and alone. I was interested to hear later how people of my generation had cried as memories of the war were vividly revived during the lockdown.

During this time, I received two telephone calls from friends whose husbands had died. In both cases, only six people were allowed to go to the funerals.

The months rolled by, and I had been isolated for nearly a year. Chocky had become used to not going out for walks, he adapted to getting his exercise by racing up and down the patio whenever a swan or cormorant was swimming by.

I decided that—despite the warning from the consultant to still keep away from other people—I would risk a little walk alongside the marina when it was quiet. I felt really nervous even getting my powered chair out, and was shaking when I reached the other side of the marina where the footpath was.

One or two people came along and I quickly moved away, this was so alien to me as I was used to going up to people, especially, those with dogs, and talking with them. How I longed for human contact.

After a further nine weeks, I started to go out every day, often at dusk when it was quiet; just to remind myself that there was a world outside. Tendai came back to help me, but Rue never returned from Zimbabwe.

Over the Rainbow

The rainbow postcards which hung in people's windows were now fading. A year had passed, and spring, summer, autumn, and winter merged into one long season. Christmas had gone, empty and fragmented, and the New Year slipped into January almost unnoticed.

But there was one great turning point, the introduction of Covid vaccinations. Queues of people could be seen patiently waiting outside surgeries and pharmacies. What a blessing they were. Gradually, slowly, and little by little, the government relaxed some rules.

Families could meet outside in groups of six known as bubbles, as long as they wore masks, did not touch one another and, continuously, washed their hands. People could travel in their cars, initially limited to one county. Shops began to open with precautions.

Children gradually returned to school but had to wear masks and sit two metres apart. Churches were allowed to open again provided they followed the rules of wearing masks, washing hands, sitting apart and not touching anyone.

Meanwhile, every hospital was overflowing with Covid casualties and hundreds of people were dying. I remained alone at home for 15 months, apart from taking Chocky out for short walks. There was no family bubble for me to join in.

But my friend Vivienne—whom I had worked with in counselling for over 30 years—invited me to visit her. It was a strange meeting. I had not seen her for so long, and yet I had to keep away from her. We could not touch and had to wash our hands both at the beginning and end of my visit.

After many more weeks, I decided to go to church and play for a service. This was a huge step to take. The words of the consultant and the letter I had received from the N.H.S.—telling me to stay indoors and keep safe because I was vulnerable—kept ringing in my ears.

I thought I would be full of joy, at last, I would meet in person the friends I had only seen on Zoom for so long. But it was very different. A cloak of fear and anxiety seemed to wrap around me as I stepped out of the car. I felt weak. My hands trembled as I put on my mask, and my legs shook as slowly I walked through the door.

So many called out greetings of love and welcome, but I could touch no one. I longed to give each one a hug. I wandered down to the piano, got out my music, sat down and started to play. I was facing the congregation, it looked strange, everyone was sitting with two chairs between them, their faces half-covered with masks.

I was unable to recognise some. It was almost impossible to sing the hymns. I played as positively as I could, but the minister almost sang a solo as she was the only one not wearing a mask. I felt emotionally numb and returned home exhausted and confused.

Gradually, life in general returned to a new normal. We had found a little of the blue sky beyond the rainbow.

Three years have now passed, during which, a hospital consultant arranged an echocardiogram for me. It took much longer than expected, and when I asked why, they told me they could not find my heart!

It was eventually located on the right side of my body and reversed, but still beating well! This would account for the complications which arose during the surgery I had while at college over 60 years ago; science and technology have improved so much since then.

A pacemaker was inserted unusually on the right side. Unfortunately, I never regained the strength I had before those long months of isolation, and have not been able to return to the activities I had previously so enjoyed.

I noticed little Chocky was beginning to walk more slowly. At first, I thought it was possibly his age, but decided to take him to the vet for a check-up. He was given a scan, and sadly, it showed he had a tumour on his bladder.

I took him to the Cambridge Animal Hospital every two weeks for chemotherapy, Tendai drove us there, and he was a tremendous support. To our disappointment, there was no improvement after six months, and after very careful thought and discussions with the consultant, it was decided to end his suffering.

Little Chocky lay in my arms on a fleecy blanket. He was quite comfortable and at peace. As the syringe was inserted, he licked the consultant's hand as if to say *thank you*. We both had tears in our eyes. He had been such a faithful little companion throughout such a difficult time.

The apartment was now silent again; a deep silence, empty and lonely. In my life, I have only had approximately eight weeks without a dog. I began to look on the internet, I would have loved another Yorkshire Terrier but could not find one in my area needing a home. I have always had rescue dogs.

A friend suggested I look for a Chihuahua as they were easy to feed and needed very little exercise. She then found one for me on Facebook, a 10-year-old whose owner was unwell. Binki was one of 12 chihuahuas used for breeding.

Sadly, all her pups had died. My nephew drove me to Nottinghamshire and there she was, curled up in a corner surrounded by a multitude of barking dogs. I had to take her. Binki has been a very loveable, affectionate little companion for a year now.

Unfortunately, she objects to strangers and nips anyone who tries to come in—which is not always helpful. Once she knows someone, she is fine and a tiny, loveable friend to me.

***

It is late afternoon. The early spring sun is setting and the glory of its radiant light is mirrored in the water of the marina alongside my patio. Seagulls circle and swoop above, flying against the background of fresh green trees.

A cormorant plops into the water, disappears, then, rises again in the shadow of the reeds. Six swans, a mother, a father and four tiny grey cygnets softly paddle their way downstream. A collared dove sits silently on my patio railings, and a moorhen quietly pecks at a few seeds for his supper.

The sun sinks lower, the colours fade and darkness falls. All is still, all is calm, and another day will soon be over. This beauty sustains me day by day, it is always there, even in the rain; a tranquil reminder that there is still peace in this troubled world.

I am so privileged to be part of it. May polio gradually be eradicated throughout the whole world and never return to the British Isles as immunisation faithfully continues and parents ensure their children are vaccinated.

My final words are to anyone with a disability:

"Never lose hope. Always believe in yourself, never give up, and do not be afraid to reach out as far as you are able to. Explore the wonders of this world and life. I celebrated my 90th birthday in 2024, and as I look back remembering all the different experiences I have had, and the many lovely people I have met, I quietly smile."

"They said, I would never work!"